THE IMPATIENT GOURMET / *Isabel Jones*

WW

WILLIAM WATERMAN PUBLICATIONS

Kellogg's

Published by William Waterman Publications
A division of William Waterman Publications (Pty) Ltd
PO Box 5091
Rivonia
2128

First published by Penguin Books in 1990

Acknowledgements
Grateful thanks to Hilary Biller for assistance in the compilation of recipes, and to Spilhaus for the loan of china and glassware.
® Registered Trademarks of the Kellogg's Company.
Styling by Isabel Jones.

ISBN 0 9583751 6 X

Typeset by Press Books, Johannesburg with additional typesetting by Photoprints, Cape Town
Printed and bound by ABC Book Printers, Cape Town
Cover design by Anton Sassenberg

To my husband Barry — a critical trencherman
who is sparing with praise
but who will never moan at a burnt offering.

INTRODUCTION

I was going to call this book *The Impatient Cook* but decided that it smacked too much of instant soup cooking. Whereas the Impatient *Gourmet* will be prepared for a bit of cooking aggro if it can be justified — and I will justify home-made mayonnaise with my last breath!

The Impatient Gourmet comes rushing home, starving, but doesn't always want to eat gourmet take-aways or frozen offerings. It is to this person — male or female — that this book is dedicated.

Having come from a home where Mother was a lousy cook (all the meats looked grey and all the vegetables yellow), I learnt to cook as a matter of survival. I love to eat and can never understand people not enjoying their own cooking. As I stir a sauce I'm busy, mentally, licking my lips. The Cordon Bleu School in London helped to train me in the proper ways of doing things but I like to think that I'm also good at finding short cuts. Life is not too short to stuff a mushroom — as long as you know that you use a piping bag without a nozzle (because you do it at lightning speed without getting the stuffing all over the counter, your arms and your shoes).

Some recipes take a little longer than others — after all everyone has to entertain sometimes. But do give all the recipes a try. I'm hoping that you are going to like them.

Happy eating!

P.S. To all those less-than-sylph-like eager eaters, herewith my favourite saying: Never trust a skinny cook!

GET YOURSELF ORGANISED…

Every Impatient Gourmet needs a few kitchen genies.

- If you haven't got a food processor, it's a must. It revolutionised the commercial kitchen — let it revolutionise yours. It cuts hours off chopping, grating, slicing, blending, mixing. And it has the blessing of being super-quick and easy to wash up. I once counted and found I had used mine (and washed it up) 9 times during one big 'cook-in'.

- I was a late-comer to the microwave but am now one of its top fans. I do *not* use it for everything. I still like to cook my meats in the oven, but the microwave cuts hours off specific cooking tasks. It does so many jobs quickly, efficiently and cost effectively. You can time fish and vegetables to seconds — you just need to get to know your particular machine's timings and idiosyncrasies. See the footnote on page 2 for information on the microwave oven used to test the recipes in this book.

- If you already have a microwave, invest in some efficient jugs and dishes. Some containers sold under a microwave-proof label are hopelessly inefficient. They absorb too many of the microwaves themselves. Do a test by putting 250 ml water in a glass jug and placing it in the dish you want to test. Microwave on full power for 1 minute. The water should be warm and the dish cool. If it is the other way round, change the dish. Round dishes are better than rectangular ones.

- If you are really into cooking, invest in a large mixer with a moving beater (as opposed to the smaller type where the bowl moves round). They do a far superior job and have K-beater attachments for pastry-making and a dough hook for breads.

- You must have good quality razor-sharp knives. And don't keep them in a drawer. It blunts them. And don't plonk them into the washing-up bowl. That also blunts them. Wipe them after use and put them into a knife block or on a magnetic rack. One gadget which I love is an electric knife grinder and polisher from America. Do keep your knives sharp. More people cut themselves with blunt knives than with sharp ones.

Get yourself kitted up with efficient kitchen aids. After all, no one expects an accountant still to use the quill. Life in the kitchen gets pleasanter when some of the slog is removed. If you enjoy eating, learn to enjoy cooking.

Amaretto Cream with Plum Purée

Depending on the sweetness of your tooth, the sugar content can be as low as 30 ml or as high as 60 ml. A little Amaretto can be added to the plum purée to make it extra special.

By the way, ramekins are small straight-sided ovenproof dishes — just the size for a single serving.

300 g ricotta cheese
300 ml yoghurt
45 ml castor sugar
90 ml Amaretto
20 ml gelatine
1 x 400 g can plums
flaked almonds, toasted

Beat the ricotta cheese, yoghurt and sugar together until smooth. Place 45 ml of the Amaretto in a small saucepan and shake the gelatine over the surface of the liqueur until it has been absorbed. Leave for a minute or two until the gelatine has turned into a 'cake'. Put over a low heat until the mixture turns transparent — it is important that it does not boil. Stir into the ricotta/yoghurt mixture.

Add the rest of the Amaretto and stir. Spoon into small, individual ramekins or moulds which have been oiled and lined with a little piece of greaseproof paper for easy removal. Cover with cling wrap and refrigerate until set.

Drain the plums and remove the stones. Purée the fruit and refrigerate until required.

To serve, dip each mould into hot water for a few seconds. Loosen the edges of the cream with a small palette knife and allow air to get into the mould, turning it all the way round. Turn out on to small plates, pour the plum purée around the base of the cream and decorate with the flaked almonds.

If you do not wish to unmould, place the ramekin on a plate (you can use a dreaded doily if you want to) with a beautiful leaf or flower. It makes good visual impact.

Makes 6-8 servings, depending on the size of the ramekins or moulds.

Apple and Cointreau Pots

1 kg fresh green apples, peeled and chopped
2 oranges, rind and pulp, finely chopped
225 g brown sugar (or less, depending on sharpness of oranges)
Cointreau
375 ml cream, whipped
75 ml slivered almonds

Put the apples in a pan with the chopped orange rind and pulp and just enough water to cover them. Simmer gently, uncovered, for 15 minutes. Stir in the sugar and continue to cook over low heat until most of the liquid has been absorbed and the apples are cooked.

Allow to cool. Purée. Add Cointreau to taste, stir in the whipped cream and slivered almonds. Pour into ramekins and chill.

Serves 4-6.

Stuffed Apple Salad

4 Golden Delicious apples
2 sticks celery, finely chopped
60 ml thick cream
10 ml lemon juice
1 clove garlic, crushed
little castor sugar
freshly ground black pepper
walnuts for garnish

Cut the tops off the apples. Using a grapefruit spoon, scoop out the flesh without breaking the skin of the apples. Remove cores and seeds. Chop finely and place in a bowl. Add the celery and then mix in the cream, lemon juice, garlic, sugar and seasonings. Don't stir the dressing too vigorously or it will curdle. The apple and celery should be nicely coated. Spoon into the apple cases and decorate with a walnut half.

Serve with triangles of cheese pastry (see p 54).

Serves 4.

Asparagus and Cheese Charlotte

Wonderful for Sunday supper. This is the savoury version of the old favourite, bread and butter pudding.

8 slices brown bread
butter
1 x 300g can asparagus spears, well drained, or fresh cooked asparagus in season
175 g Cheddar cheese, grated
3 jumbo eggs
550 ml milk
salt and freshly ground black pepper
pinch of dry mustard

Butter one side of each slice of bread and cut 4 slices to fit a buttered, ovenproof dish. The buttered side should be uppermost. Layer with the asparagus spears, and half the grated cheese. Cover with the remaining bread, butter side down. In a separate bowl, beat together the eggs, milk, salt, pepper and mustard. Pour over the bread in the dish, soaking it well.

Leave the dish to stand for 15-30 minutes. This is to ensure that the custard soaks into the bread. Sprinkle the remaining cheese on top of the bread. Bake in a preheated oven at 180°C for about 35-45 minutes.

4 generous servings.

Asparagus with Yoghurt Dressing

Makes a simple but elegant dinner starter.

Trim a bunch of fresh asparagus and place in a roasting bag with a spoonful of water, a knob of butter and a little salt. Tie the neck of the bag (don't use metal) and microwave* on full power — the time taken will depend on the quantity and thickness of the asparagus. I use full power for 3 minutes for a bunch of the thinnish green variety.

Meanwhile make the dressing by mixing together

175 ml thick plain yoghurt
grated rind of 1 lemon
15 ml chopped chives

This makes sufficient dressing for 4 servings.

Place the asparagus on a plate with a serving of dressing next to it. Sprinkle grated or desiccated coconut on top of the dressing. Garnish with a slice of lemon.

Baked Avocados

A pleasant winter starter.

500 ml white sauce (see p 64)
15 ml tomato paste
15 ml grated onion
15 ml butter
15 ml curry powder
1 x 230g can crab meat (or crab sticks, at a pinch)
2 ripe avocados
juice of 1 lemon

Mix together the white sauce, tomato paste, grated onion, butter and curry powder. Fold in the flaked crab meat and heat the mixture until just below boiling point. Do not let the mixture boil.

Cut the avocados in half and put the cut side in lemon juice for a minute to prevent discoloration. Fill the avocados with the crab mixture and place in a casserole containing 2,5 cm of boiling water. Cover with lid. Bake at 170°C for 20 minutes.

Serves 4.

---

* **Note:** All microwave recipes in this book were tested in a 600 watt microwave oven. If your microwave is of a higher wattage, decrease the cooking time slightly, but if it is of a lower wattage you will need to increase the cooking time.

Avocado with Blue Cheese Dressing

Wonderful as a starter or a light luncheon.

60 g Roquefort or any blue cheese
30 ml cream
45 ml French dressing or sherry dressing (see p 31)
Worcestershire sauce
grated nutmeg
2 avocados
lettuce
spring onions

Put the cheese in a bowl and soften with a fork. Gradually add the cream and blend to a paste. Slowly add enough French dressing to give a coating consistency. Add a few drops of Worcestershire sauce and a pinch of nutmeg. Just before serving halve, stone and peel the avocados. Slice thickly and arrange on lettuce leaves. Spoon the dressing over the avocado and garnish with snipped spring onion tops or chives.

Serves 4.

Avocado Guacamole

(Illustrated on page 9)

This makes an excellent informal starter which can be passed round with Toast Melba (p 73) or julienne (large matchsticks) of carrot, celery and cucumber. I usually make it when I am cooking Paella (p 54) on the braai. Everyone eats it while they stand round chatting and drinking.

3 ripe avocados
juice of 1 large lemon
2 cloves garlic, crushed
4 tomatoes, skinned, seeded and cut into slivers
2,5 ml chilli powder (make certain it is fresh)
1 bunch spring onions, chopped
1 stick celery, finely chopped
1 small green pepper, seeded and finely sliced
30 ml parsley, chopped
50 ml oil
salt and freshly ground black pepper

Skin the avocados and then mash them with the lemon juice. Add the rest of the ingredients and stir. Make sure that you add sufficient salt and freshly ground black pepper. Leave one of the avocado stones in the mixture until ready to serve — it prevents discoloration of the avocado. Cover with cling wrap and chill.

Serves 6-8.

To remove the skins of tomatoes easily, place on paper towel in the microwave. Cover with paper towel and microwave on full power for approximately 30 seconds. Leave to stand for a few minutes and then skin.

Avocado Mousse

3 large ripe avocados
6 spring onions, chopped coarsely
150 ml mayonnaise
150 ml smooth cottage cheese (if you are feeling rich, use Philadelphia cream cheese or, as an alternative, use 100 ml smooth cottage cheese blended with 50 ml blue cheese)
15-20 ml gelatine (depending on whether you want to unmould the mousse or not)
150 ml chicken stock
salt and freshly ground black pepper
few drops Tabasco sauce

Mash the avocados and mix with the spring onions, mayonnaise and cheese. This can be done in a food processor if you like the onions liquidised. Take 45 ml of the *cold* (this is vital) stock and place in a small ramekin (for microwave) or baby saucepan (for the top of thc stove). Sprinkle the measured gelatine on to the stock and shake constantly until it has been absorbed. Leave for 1 minute to turn into a 'cake'. Microwave for about 30 seconds or place on the lowest heat on the top of the stove until it becomes translucent. Do not let it boil. Add to the avocado and onion mixture, stirring well as gelatine has a tendency to sink unless properly mixed in. Add the rest of the stock and the seasonings.

I like to set this mousse in an oiled ring mould. I place a few pieces of oiled baking paper round the base of the mould to ensure easy removal. Cover the mould with cling wrap and chill. When set, loosen carefully around the edge with a palette knife, letting air into the mould as you move it around. Invert over a serving dish and give a mighty shake.

Garnish with chopped skinned tomato (over the top) or fresh herbs. Alternatively, place a big bunch of watercress in the centre.

Serves 6 generously and 8 elegantly.

Brazilian Bananas

This is a dessert quickie, so simple but so delicious.

8 bananas
30 ml dark rum
250 ml cream
90 ml sugar
20 ml instant coffee
a few browned slivered almonds

Peel the bananas and slice thickly. Sprinkle with the rum. Whip the cream and fold in the sugar and coffee. Cover the bananas with this mixture.

Sprinkle with the slivered almonds. Chill well before serving.

Serves 6.

Old-Fashioned Baked Beans with Ham Chunks

3 x 400g cans baked beans
1 large onion, chopped
3 tomatoes, peeled and chopped
60 ml molasses or treacle
250 ml ham, cut into chunks
salt and pepper
60 ml dark brown sugar
1 x 400g can pineapple rings

Mix the baked beans, onion, tomatoes, molasses, ham and seasonings together. Place in a casserole. The traditionalists insist that it should be an earthenware one.

Sprinkle the brown sugar over the top. Bake in a preheated oven at 180°C for approximately 1½ hours or until the mixture has glazed.

Garnish with rings of canned pineapple.

Serves 4.

Corned Beef Hash

If you have left-over cabbage — and even creamed potatoes — from Sunday lunch, this makes a wonderfully easy Monday evening supper. The traditional accompaniment to this dish is a fried egg on each serving.

1 x 300g can corned beef
1 packet instant mashed potato (made according to instructions on the packet)
2 large onions, finely sliced
about 200 g cooked cabbage
125 ml beef stock
15 ml tomato paste
sprinkling of sugar
salt and freshly ground black pepper
oil and butter

Mix the corned beef with the potato, breaking up the corned beef. Meanwhile, gently fry the onion in a little oil and butter until soft but not brown. Add to the corned beef mixture together with the cabbage (I particularly like the baby cabbage), beef stock, tomato paste, the lightest sprinkling of sugar, salt (go easy if you have used instant stock) and freshly ground black pepper. (It *must* be black pepper to give that wonderfully flavourful bite.)

If you are a curry addict, a sprinkling of curry powder can be added to the pan after cooking the onions. 'Mellow' for a minute or two before adding to the corned beef mixture.

Heat a little oil with some butter in a frying pan and add the mixture, spreading it out well so that the base can become crusty. Cook over a medium heat but do not fiddle with it. It is vital for the base to set and brown.

In an ideal world you would have another frying pan ready when it is time to turn the hash so that you can flop it in and make the upper side crusty. Impatient Cooks won't be bothered so use 2 fish-slices and try to flip it over fairly undamaged. This process of browning and heating the mixture through will take at least 15 minutes on each side.

Serves 4.

Fillet of Beef

The beauty of serving fillet is that you don't have to battle if you are an inadequate carver. You can also rely on the meat being tender, and there are no hidden bones to take into account when you are calculating the number of servings.

1 whole fillet of beef
45 ml oil
45 ml butter
salt and freshly ground black pepper
streaky bacon

Remove all the membrane from the fillet. Heat the oil in a large frying pan and add the butter. When it is foaming add the fillet. Brown it thoroughly on all sides, sealing it well. Remove from the pan and season well.

Wrap the streaky bacon round the fillet like a bandage, overlapping just a little so that the fillet is totally covered.

Transfer to a roasting pan and cook in a preheated oven at 220°C for approximately 25-35 minutes, depending on how thick the fillet is and how rare you like your beef. Serve with a béarnaise sauce (see p 62).

Should serve 8.

Fillet of Beef with Mustard Sauce

1 fillet of beef
marinade:
60 ml grainy French mustard
60 ml soft brown sugar
30 ml Worcestershire sauce
15 ml mushroom sauce (if you can get it)
40 ml red wine vinegar
60 ml melted butter
for sauce:
125 ml thick cream

Trim the fillet by removing any membrane. Mix the marinade ingredients together. Place the meat and the marinade in a large plastic bag and rest in a dish (to avoid spilling). Chill in the fridge for 4-5 hours, turning the meat in the marinade occasionally. Drain the meat but reserve the marinade. Cook the meat in a very hot oven, preheated to 220°C, for 25-35 minutes, depending on the size and thickness of the fillet.

Meanwhile, heat the marinade in a small pan and simmer for a few minutes. Add the cream and cook for a further 2-3 minutes.

When the fillet is cooked, slice and top with the sauce. Serve with baked potatoes and salad.

Should serve 8.

Roast Beef and Delicious Gravy

There's something very traditional about a delicious roast for Sunday lunch.

I have very strong views on Roast Beef — it has got to be on the bone. It tastes so much better that I don't care if it makes the carving more difficult.

Granny liked to rub dry mustard over the joint, as it sat on the kitchen counter. She didn't have a fridge, but you do. So *never* take the meat straight from the fridge to the oven. Let it 'come to' at room temperature.

John Tovey taught me to rub the joint with a little curry powder. It doesn't actually give the final result a hot flavour. It merely enhances it and gives the gravy a divine taste. So try either mustard or curry — it's up to you.

Turn the oven on to maximum. Most experts feel that the slow cooking method stops shrinkage, but I prefer a bit of shrinkage and more flavour. Heat the baking dish in the oven. Chop an onion into 4, but do not remove the skin. The onion skin helps to colour the gravy so that you don't have to resort to trickery. Pop the meat into the very hot oven dish and turn it around to seal. If the meat has a nice layer of lovely yellowy fat (and at my dear old Cordon Bleu School in London we were taught that fat is the flavour house of meat), leave it topwards so that it bastes the meat as it cooks.

Put the meat with the onion into the oven at top temperature for 15 minutes. Reduce the heat to 220°C and cook for 15 minutes per 450 g (total cooking time), basting from time to time with the juices. This timing is for rare beef. Continue cooking if your preferences are for medium or well cooked beef.

Beef gravy should be thin. Remove the joint to a serving dish, and keep warm. Pour off most of the fat from the juices. Add just a sprinkling of flour to absorb the grease and juices. Return to the heat and cook the flour mixture until it is brown (to give colour to the gravy). Add 5 ml tomato paste, a tiny pinch of sugar, a shake of Worcestershire sauce, 30 ml red wine and strained cooking water of any green vegetables you are serving. Simmer. Season well with salt and freshly ground black pepper — do remember that the vegetable water has already been salted. It's vital to simmer the gravy to 'mellow' the flavours. If it still tastes a bit harsh, add a further sprinkling of sugar.

I can't bear lukewarm gravy so, having got it just right, I strain it into a microwave jug and leave it to stand. Just before serving, I give it a quick blast on full power in the microwave to have it really hot.

(Tomato paste acts as a thickener. If you think it is extravagant to open a can of tomato paste for just a teaspoon, remember that you can pop it into the freezer and then scrape out a further spoonful, still frozen, the next time you need it.)

Boeuf Stroganoff

This is the ideal Impatient Gourmet's recipe. And before you keel over at the price of beef fillet, remember there is no waste and a little goes a long way. The only danger with this dish is that it can easily be ruined by overcooking the beef.

500 g fillet of beef
15 ml oil
30 ml butter
1 onion, finely chopped
250 g mushrooms, sliced
100 ml dry white wine
150 ml beef stock
15 ml oil
30 ml butter
30 ml brandy
125 - 175 ml cream
rind and juice of 1 lemon
15 ml chopped parsley
salt and freshly ground black pepper

The biggest pain with this dish is cutting the meat. The pieces should be cut to the size of a double matchstick! But that's the worst part.

Heat the first 15 ml oil and 30 ml butter together and sauté the onion until soft but not brown. Add the mushrooms and toss for 1-2 minutes. Add the wine and beef stock and reduce until just about 3-4 tablespoons of liquid remain. Scrape into a bowl.

Heat the next 15 ml oil and 30 ml butter until very hot and quickly, quickly, seal the slivers of beef. Pour in the brandy. Ignite. Shake the pan until the flames die down. Add the onion and mushroom mixture, taking care to scrape every flavourful bit back into the pan. Add the cream, lemon rind and juice, parsley and seasonings. Simmer for a minute. Serve immediately.

Serves 4-6 people.

Brandy Butter

Great with Christmas pud, cake or mince pies.

125 g butter
125 g sifted icing sugar
45 ml brandy (or sherry — at a pinch)

Cream the butter vigorously until it is light in colour. Add the sifted icing sugar gradually, beating continuously. When the mixture is light and fluffy, add the brandy — a few drops at a time — beating continuously, until all the brandy has been blended into the mixture. If you prefer a sweeter mixture, double the sugar content.

Brandy Truffles

125 g dark chocolate
125 g sweet butter (unsalted)
275 g icing sugar, sifted
30 ml brandy
chocolate vermicelli
cocoa
browned nibs of almonds

Melt the chocolate by placing in a microwave bowl, cover with cling wrap and microwave on medium power for approximately $3^1/_2$ minutes (depending on the type of bowl and the power of the microwave). Stir half-way through.

Cream the butter and gradually add the icing sugar, beating well until light and fluffy. Add the melted chocolate to the butter and sugar mixture and beat well. Flavour with the brandy. Allow to cool.

Take teaspoonfuls of the mixture and roll in the hands to form balls. Then coat the truffles in chocolate vermicelli, cocoa or browned nibs of almonds. The quickest way to do this is to place both coating and rolled truffle in an egg-cup and shake until the truffle is completely covered. Place each truffle in a small paper cup and store in the refrigerator.

They look very attractive if you have used the three different coatings. Very fattening but quite delicious. Need I say more?

Bread

Easy Bread

So easy! Eat it on the day that it is made.

500 g self-raising flour
5 ml salt
340 ml (1 dumpy) beer

Sift the flour and salt into a bowl. Pour in the beer. Stir until well mixed and place in a small greased bread tin.

Bake in a preheated oven at 180°C for 50-55 minutes.

Easy Yoghurt Loaf

This loaf is absolutely delicious and very easy to make.

200 g crushed wheat
175 g wholewheat flour
125 g fresh wheatgerm
5 ml bicarbonate of soda
10 ml salt
30 ml honey
500 ml thick yoghurt
natural sesame seeds

Mix the wheat, flour, wheatgerm, bicarb and salt together in a large bowl. Add the honey and the yoghurt and stir well. Place in a greased loaf tin and sprinkle with the sesame seeds. Bake at 180°C for $1^1/_4$ - $1^1/_2$ hours.

Spicy Marmalade Bread

This is a wonderful idea for a brunch party.

Cut a French loaf into 3 cm diagonal slices. Spread with softened butter. Then spread with a generous helping of marmalade. Sprinkle ground cinnamon over the top and bake in a preheated oven at 200°C, marmalade side up, for about 4 minutes.

Opposite: Avocado Guacamole
Overleaf: Burgers Stroganoff
Prepared with choice ingredients from Woolworths food markets

Burgers Stroganoff

(Illustrated on page 10)

When I did some research for a television programme on The Burger, I came across an interesting tale — which I firmly believe. In the early 1850s many people were emigrating from Hamburg to New York. A speciality of Hamburg at that time was a dried beef — it sounds a bit like biltong — which would survive the refrigerator-less voyage and would suit the Jewish steerage passengers. To make it more palatable on the long journey, the chefs minced it and mixed it with minced onion and breadcrumbs soaked in water. The resulting patties were then fried. When the passengers reached the New World, they went on making the 'Hamburg patties', but with fresh minced meat. Hence the hamburger and not the beefburger!

8 hamburger patties
1 onion, finely chopped
60 g butter
125 g mushrooms, sliced
10 ml tomato paste
pinch of sugar
300 ml cream
45 ml lemon juice
100 ml beef stock

These quantities will make sufficient sauce for 8 hamburgers.

Sauté the onion in the butter until soft but not brown — this can be done on top of the stove or in the microwave. Add the mushrooms and cook for 2-3 minutes. Stir in the tomato paste and the sugar. Cook for a minute. Add the cream, lemon juice and stock, stirring well. Simmer.

Meanwhile grill or fry the burgers. When cooked, cut into strips, add to the sauce and heat for a minute or two.

4 servings.

C

Savoury Cabbage

This is easy to make if you have a food processor — the miracle kitchen machine!

60 g butter
700 g young cabbage, finely shredded
1 medium onion, grated
3 rashers streaky bacon, chopped
pinch of fresh ground nutmeg

Heat the butter in a large pan. Add all the ingredients and cover with a lid. Cook very gently for 10 - 20 minutes, shaking the pan occasionally.

Serves 4-6, depending on how much you like cabbage.

Charlotte Katrine

This outstanding dessert originated in the kitchen of the Old Edwardian Club in Johannesburg, but I have modified it slightly over the years. If almond nibs aren't available, just chop whole blanched ones — in the food processor of course.

The quantities given below will fill a 15 cm cake tin (preferably one with a removable bottom), which should be lined with either greaseproof or baking paper. If you are having a very big dinner party, double the quantities and use a 20-23 cm cake tin.

125 g dark chocolate
125 g butter
50 g castor sugar
125 g almond nibs
175 ml thick cream

to decorate:
boudoir biscuits
cream and chocolate
strawberries, if available

Melt the chocolate in the microwave (see p 17 for method), or in the top of a double-boiler, or in a basin over a pan of simmering water.

Meanwhile, beat the butter until light and fluffy. Add the sugar, continuing to beat well. Stir in the almonds and the melted chocolate.

Lightly whip the cream until it starts thickening. If you are lucky enough to have thick yellow cream, don't even bother to beat it. The cream should be thick but still pourable. Stir it into the chocolate mixture.

(If you have beaten the cream until almost piping texture, don't worry. It will still taste good but as it is almost impossible to mix thick cream in properly you will get a marbled effect — which actually looks quite good.)

Spoon the mixture into the prepared cake tin. Cover and refrigerate. You can do this stage a couple of days before you need it.

Unmould the charlotte on to a serving dish. It really does make life so much easier if the tin has a removable base as the charlotte can then easily be pushed out of the tin. Measure one boudoir biscuit against the side of the charlotte and then trim it at one end so that it is just slightly higher (about the height of a finger-nail) than the charlotte. Using this boudoir biscuit as your measure, cut enough biscuits to go all the way round the charlotte. Take some stiffly beaten cream and spread a little on the inside of each biscuit. The cream will anchor the biscuits in an upright position against the side of the charlotte.

If you want a grand effect, take some wide ribbon and tie it around the charlotte — outside the biscuits, of course. Or if, like me, you can never tie a bow properly, use a pearl-headed pin to secure the two ends of the ribbon decoratively. The pin will easily go into the biscuits, holding the ribbon tight and firm. It's easily removed before serving.

Pipe or spoon some whipped cream into the centre of the cake and decorate with chocolate leaves (see p 18) or curls. Chocolate curls are made by running a swivel potato peeler down the side of a bar of chocolate which has been warmed by hand. Pipe rosettes of cream around the base of the cake and decorate with strawberries, if available, and more chocolate curls.

Charlotte Katrine must be served well chilled.

6-8 portions. It is very rich!

Cheese and Bacon Potato Cakes

1 onion
30 ml oil
100 g bacon
60 g cheese
left-over mashed potato — about the quantity of 2 large potatoes
salt and pepper
little additional oil for frying

Slice the onion finely and fry in the oil until soft but not brown. Cut the bacon into slivers and fry until crisp.

Grate the cheese and add with the mashed potato to the pan, stirring well. Season with salt and pepper.

Divide the mixture into four and form into flat patties. Fry in a clean frying pan in a little hot oil until golden and crunchy on both sides.

Serve with baked beans, sausages and tomato for a delicious Sunday evening supper. Or, alternatively, top with a fried egg.

Makes 2 generous servings.

Shirley's Cheesecake

This is a super recipe for cheesecake from my friend, Shirley Kilian.

1 packet digestive biscuits
80 g butter, melted
2,5 ml ground cinnamon
500 ml cream
1 x 397 g can condensed milk
225 ml fresh lemon juice
fresh fruit to garnish

Put the biscuits in a plastic bag and use a rolling pin to crush them or quickly grind them in a food processor. Mix with the butter and the cinnamon. Line a serving dish with the biscuit base.

Beat the cream until it begins to thicken and add the condensed milk and stir. Add the lemon juice. It should thicken well. Pour the mixture on top of the biscuit base and chill.

The dessert can be frozen at this stage. In fact, on one occasion, in an emergency, Shirley served it frozen as an ice-cream dish which tasted absolutely delicious.

Just before serving, decorate with fruit.

Serves 8.

P.S. Yes, we do know there is no cheese in it!

Cherries Jubilee

1 x 425 g can black cherries
30 ml sugar
1 stick cinnamon
juice and grated rind of 1 orange
10 ml cornflour
60 ml brandy
vanilla ice-cream

Drain the cherries and reserve the juice. Add the sugar to the cinnamon, orange juice and rind and most of the black cherry juice. Use the rest of the cherry juice to mix with the cornflour.

Bring the sugar/juice mixture to the boil and add the cornflour, stirring well. Cook for a couple of minutes, stirring, and then add the cherries to warm through. Remove the cinnamon stick.

Heat the brandy in a small separate pan and ignite. Pour over the cherry mixture and when the flames die down, pour over individual servings of vanilla ice-cream.

Serves 4.

Chicken Hotpot

A tasty family dish which is also nice cold.

1 chicken, jointed into 8 pieces
45 ml flour
salt and freshly ground black pepper
45 ml oil
30 ml butter
2 onions, slices
1 x 400 g can tomatoes, drained well and sliced
2 cloves garlic, crushed
1 bay leaf

Toss the chicken pieces in flour which has been seasoned with salt and pepper. Heat the oil in a large frying pan and add the butter. Fry the chicken pieces until golden brown on all sides — it takes longer than you think. Remove the chicken pieces and fry the onions until soft but not brown. Add a little of the seasoned flour to absorb the fat. Stir well. Add the canned tomatoes and juice, together with the garlic and bay leaf. Stir again. Bring to the boil and return the chicken pieces to the pan. Season well. Cover with a tightly-fitting lid and simmer for 30 minutes, or until the chicken is cooked.

The gravy can be thickened with a little cornflour slaked with some cold water. Bring back to the boil and cook for a few minutes, stirring well, to mellow the flavour of the cornflour.

Delicious served with hot cooked pasta and a side dish of buttered courgettes.

Serves 4.

Chicken Moroccan

If you haven't got a steamer, use a large metal sieve inside a saucepan and cover with a dome of foil. Take care to secure the foil firmly round the edge of the pan so that the steam doesn't escape.

1 large chicken
salt
125 g couscous, cooked (see p 23)
75 g seedless raisins, soaked in brandy
100 g almonds, slivered
butter
2,5 ml ground cinnamon
2,5 ml cayenne pepper
freshly ground black pepper
salt
sugar

Rub the chicken with salt. Place the cooked couscous in a large mixing bowl. Add the raisins. Meanwhile sauté the almonds in a little butter until golden brown. Add to the bowl together with the cinnamon, cayenne pepper, black pepper, salt and a little sugar.

Stuff the chicken with this mixture — the easy way to do it is to use a piping bag without a nozzle. Just insert the bag into the chicken and squeeze the stuffing into the cavity.

Secure the chicken flap with poultry pins, or sew with string. Place the chicken in the upper part of a steamer and cover with buttered greaseproof paper. Steam for approximately 1½ hours. It is vital to keep the bottom pan of the steamer three-quarters full of boiling liquid, which can be either stock or water.

Serves 6.

Chicken with Oranges

A most interesting combination of flavours.

1 chicken, jointed into 8 portions
salt and pepper
pinch of ground cinnamon
pinch of ground cloves
45 ml oil
1 medium-sized onion, chopped
2 cloves garlic, crushed
250 ml orange juice
30 ml seedless raisins
15 ml capers
orange slices for garnish

Lightly sprinkle the chicken with salt, pepper, cinnamon and cloves. In a wide frying pan, heat the oil over medium-high heat, add the chicken portions and cook until well browned on all sides. Reserve.

Add the onion to the pan and sauté until soft but not brown. Add the garlic and cook gently for 1-2 minutes. Take care that the garlic does not burn. Return the chicken to the pan, add the orange juice, raisins and capers. Cover and simmer over low heat until the chicken is cooked (about 35 minutes).

Garnish with orange slices.

Serves 4.

Chicken and Potato Cakes

Makes an ideal family Sunday supper dish.

3 jumbo eggs
200 ml milk
125 g flour
salt and freshly ground pepper
500 g potatoes, peeled and coarsely grated
225 g onions, thinly sliced
225 g cooked chicken, cut into slivers
1 x 200 g can sweetcorn kernels, drained
45 ml oil
45 ml butter

Blend the eggs, milk, flour and seasonings together in a food processor. Chill. Meanwhile, blanch the potato and onion in boiling salted water for about 2 minutes. Drain well, taking care to press out as much liquid as possible. Stir the chicken slivers, sweetcorn, potato and onion into the chilled batter. Make certain to mix well. Heat the oil and butter in a frying pan. Spoon heaped tablespoons of the mixture into the pan. Flatten slightly and fry for about 4 minutes on each side.

This makes about 12 cakes. Once cooked keep them warm by placing them, uncovered, in a low oven. Or, use more than one pan and increase the oil and butter.

Serves 6.

Chicken Salad

A good way to use up chicken left-overs.

250 g cooked chicken, cut into cubes
1 green apple, sliced
1 red apple, sliced
2 bananas, sliced
lemon juice
250 ml cream
250 ml mayonnaise
7,5 ml curry powder
20 ml garlic chives, chopped
salt and pepper
250 g rice, cooked

Place the chicken in a bowl. Dip the apple and banana slices in lemon juice to prevent discoloration. Whip the cream until just beginning to thicken. Mix in the mayonnaise, curry powder and chopped chives. Add the apple and banana slices and a little lemon juice to the chicken and combine with the mayonnaise mixture. Mix well and season to taste. Serve with cooked rice.

Serves 4.

Chicken Tonnato

6 chicken breasts
salt and pepper
75 ml white wine
knob of butter
1 bay leaf
1 x 200 g can tuna in oil
6 anchovy fillets
30 ml lemon juice
5 ml capers
200 ml mayonnaise
freshly ground black pepper
lemon wedges

Place the chicken breasts in a casserole. Season and add wine, butter and bay leaf. Cover with foil and place in an oven preheated to 180°C for 35 minutes, or until cooked.

Meanwhile, blend the tuna, anchovy fillets, lemon juice and capers in a food processor until smooth. Mix with mayonnaise and season with black pepper.

Cut the chicken breasts, diagonally, into thin slices. Arrange on a plate. Coat with the savoury mixture. Cover and chill for 3 hours. Serve with capers and wedges of lemon.

Serves 4.

Chicken with Whisky Cream Sauce

30 g butter
5 ml Dijon mustard
4 boned chicken breasts
extra knob butter
1 medium onion, finely chopped
15 ml flour
125 ml chicken stock
125 ml cream
30 ml whisky
15 ml lemon juice
15 ml chopped parsley
salt and freshly ground black pepper

Melt the butter and mustard in a pan. Add the chicken and sauté on both sides. Cover and cook gently for 8-10 minutes. Remove the chicken and keep warm.

Add the extra butter to the pan and sauté the onion for 1 minute. Add the flour to the pan juices, and 'cook in' for a minute or two. Gradually stir in the stock and continue stirring until the sauce thickens. Then add the cream, whisky, lemon juice and parsley and simmer for a few minutes. Season to taste. Return the chicken to the pan and heat through.

Delicious with creamed potato and spinach.

Serves 4.

Chicken Liver Pâté

This is such an easy recipe. The quantity of butter used makes it a rich buttery pâté which also pipes beautifully on to canapés.

250 g chicken livers
125 g butter
1 large onion, chopped
1-2 cloves garlic, crushed
1 bay leaf
20 ml brandy
freshly ground black pepper

Check through the chicken livers to make sure that there are no green sacs which will make the pâté bitter.

Melt the butter in a pan and sauté the onion for a minute or two. Add the chicken livers, garlic and bay leaf. Cook over a moderate heat, stirring and turning occasionally. Continue cooking until the livers are *just* done — about 3-4 minutes. Add the brandy.

Remove from the heat and blend in a food processor. (Remember to remove the bay leaf.) Season with black pepper, and a little salt if necessary. Spoon into ramekins if you want individual servings, or into a larger dish. Cover with cling wrap and cool.

When cool, cover the pâté with melted butter (it melts with lightning speed in the microwave). Decorate the butter surface with some bay leaves and black peppercorns. Return to the fridge until ready for serving. Serve with Toast Melba (p 73).

Serves 4, but can be doubled, trebled ... and so on. I often make large quantities and it works just as well.

Chicken Liver Sauté

This makes a delicious light luncheon dish.

50 g streaky bacon
45 ml flour
salt and pepper
250 g chicken livers
big knob of butter
125 g rice, cooked
15 ml tomato paste
15 ml sherry
pinch of mixed herbs
125 ml chicken stock
sprinkling of sugar

Cut the bacon into slivers. Place in a small frying pan and fry until the fat starts to run. (This can also be done in the microwave.)

Place the seasoned flour in a plastic bag. Add the chicken livers and shake well until evenly coated.

Add the butter to the frying pan and heat. Add the chicken livers and cook for 3-5 minutes over a medium heat.

Remove the chicken livers from the pan. Off the stove, add the rice, tomato paste, sherry, herbs, chicken stock and sugar. Stir well. Return to the heat and simmer gently for about 5 minutes.

Return the chicken livers to the pan and gently heat through.

I love fried bread croûtons with this dish — fattening but so tasty!

Serves 4.

Devilled Chicken Liver Kebabs

Can be served as a starter or as a cocktail snack. It makes a great starter when you are braaiing.

30 ml oil
30 ml Worcestershire sauce
30 ml tomato sauce
5 ml English mustard
5 ml French mustard
5 ml sugar
salt and pepper
a dash of paprika
250 g chicken livers
streaky bacon

Mix all the ingredients together, except the chicken livers and bacon. Marinate the chicken livers in the mixture for at least 2 hours in the fridge.

Grill the chicken livers under a hot grill for 1-2 minutes on each side before wrapping with the streaky bacon. Secure with a cocktail stick and continue to grill until the bacon is crispy. Baste with the marinade.

This dish can also be braaied.

Makes a starter for 4.

Chilli Con Carne

(Illustrated on page 27)

Although Chilli con Carne was an import from America, it is now served by practically all Mexican families, who top it with avocado slices and lots of fresh coriander leaves. In fact, when I was in Mexico I found fresh coriander (and of course chillies) in everything except ice-cream.

30 ml bacon fat
1 onion, chopped
2 cloves garlic, crushed
450 g minced beef
1 x 400 g can tomatoes
2 x 400 g cans red kidney beans
15-30 ml chilli powder (depending on how hot you like it, and how fresh the chilli powder is)
5 ml oregano
2,5 ml cumin
1 bay leaf
salt and pepper
few drops Tabasco sauce

Heat the bacon fat and add the onion and garlic. Cook for a few minutes and then crumble in the minced beef, stirring well until brown. (The easiest way to do this is to squash down the mince with a potato masher.) Add the tomatoes and their liquid, the kidney beans and their liquid, chilli powder, oregano, cumin and bay leaf.

Season with salt and a little freshly ground black pepper. Add a few drops of Tabasco.

If the mixture appears a little dry, add some beef stock. Simmer uncovered, stirring occasionally, for approximately 30 minutes.

Serves 6.

Chocolate

Many recipes call for melted chocolate. Melting chocolate isn't difficult — but you need to know the rules if you don't want it to burn, go dull, or develop a white haze.

The secret of melting chocolate successfully is to keep the temperature for melting as low as possible. For this reason, microwaving is an ideal method. Break the chocolate because if it is in small pieces it will obviously take less time to melt. The easiest way to break it is to bang it on the counter while it is still in its packet. Place the pieces in a small microwave dish and cover with cling wrap. The time taken to melt the chocolate in the microwave will depend on the amount being melted and the type of dish you use. Microwave on medium for 2 minutes and stir. You will now have an idea of how quickly it is melting. If it is still solid, microwave again for 2 minutes. Otherwise try 1-minute stints.

If you don't have a microwave, place the chocolate in the top of a double-boiler or — if you haven't got a double-boiler — use a bowl that will sit inside one of your pans. When melting chocolate over simmering water, remember that the container holding the chocolate should not actually touch the water as this will make the chocolate too hot.

Chocolate Cloud

Top of the Stove and Microwave Methods

175 g dark chocolate
45 ml strong black coffee
15 ml dark rum
15 ml butter
4 eggs, separated

Top of the Stove Method
Melt the chocolate with the coffee and rum over a very low heat. Remove from the heat and beat in the butter and the egg yolks, one by one. When the yolks are added the chocolate should still be warm enough to cook them slightly, but take care that it is not too hot or the yolks will curdle.

Microwave Method
Melt the chocolate with the coffee and rum in the microwave on medium for 3 minutes. Add the butter and egg yolks and beat well. Microwave on medium for a further minute and beat. Repeat this process twice.

For both methods, the next step is to whisk the egg whites until stiff and then fold them into the chocolate mixture. Pour into wine glasses. Cover with cling wrap and chill overnight.

Top the puddings with decorative chocolate leaves. These are easily made with melted dark chocolate. Take a teaspoon of melted chocolate and trickle on to a rough outline of a leaf drawn on baking paper. Make squiggly lines (like veins) across the leaf outline. Allow to set and then peel the paper away from the chocolate leaf. (If you try to peel the chocolate away from the paper, it will break.)

Serves 6.

Chocolate Fridge Cake

It might sound lengthy but it's a quick assembly job. Break the budget and add the liqueur — it really makes a difference.

125 g dark chocolate
125 g butter
50 g icing sugar (if you have a very sweet tooth you can increase the sugar to a maximum of 100 g)
2 egg yolks (keep the whites for meringues)
150 ml thick cream
60 g almond slivers (toasted)
30 boudoir biscuits (approximately)
90 ml coffee or toffee liqueur
cream and chocolate to garnish

Melt the chocolate either in a double-boiler or in the microwave (see p 17). Whisk the butter and sugar together until light and fluffy. Add the yolks and mix well. Stir in the melted chocolate.

Whip the cream until just beginning to hold its shape. Fold the cream and the almonds into the chocolate mixture.

Line a small loaf tin with oiled paper. Line the bottom with boudoir biscuits. Sprinkle the liqueur over the biscuits. Spread some of the chocolate mixture over the biscuits. Add further layers of liqueur-sprinkled biscuits and the chocolate mixture, finishing with a layer of biscuits.

Cover with baking paper and weigh down slightly with cans. Chill in the fridge overnight.

Just before serving, turn out on to a platter and decorate with whipped cream and, if you are feeling artistic, with chocolate leaves (see above). Otherwise make chocolate curls with a swivel potato peeler run down the side of a chocolate bar heated by hand.

Serves 6.

Chocolate Ganache Cream

A must for all chocoholics. It is absolutely delicious on meringues (including almond and hazel-nut meringues) and makes a wonderful filling for sandwich cakes.

250 ml thick cream
175 g dark chocolate

Heat the cream until just simmering. Remove from the heat. Add the grated or chopped chocolate. Mix well until melted. Continue stirring over a low heat for a minute or two.

Cover and chill in the refrigerator until cold and thick.

Christmas Pudding

A home-made Christmas pudding is so easy and always tastes so much richer than the usual shop-bought one. Making your own Christmas pudding makes you feel good — sort of back-to-the-farmhouse-kitchen, even if you've always lived in a city!

This mixture will make one pud for you and one for a Christmas present for the person who has everything.

Cut down on kitchen time by buying your fruit and nuts from a specialist shop where they will weigh out the exact quantities that you need and give you the best quality ingredients.

I have conformed to the rules of ritual in the order that the ingredients are added to the mixture. But I must be honest: if you are feeling in a slapdash mood, just throw everything in higgledy-piggledy and as long as you mix thoroughly (I do it with well-scrubbed hands), the puds will turn out perfectly.

Finding a large enough mixing bowl when making lots of puddings can be difficult. Try using the sink. Make certain it is clean and dry. Use a piece of foil for the stopper. It is just the right height for stirring everything really well.

The strength of a Christmas pud is in the careful selection of ingredients. And the lengthy cooking time.

600 g seeded or seedless raisins
400 g sultanas
300 g currants
125 g mixed peel
50 g almonds, chopped or nibs
225 g fresh white breadcrumbs
225 g shredded suet (try Atora from the baking-aids section at your supermarket)
60 ml good quality marmalade
2 large lemons
225 g cake flour
pinch of salt
10 ml freshly ground nutmeg
10 ml freshly ground cinnamon
225 g soft brown sugar
275-300 ml milk stout (Guinness if possible)
3 jumbo eggs

Chop the raisins and mix with the sultanas, currants, mixed peel, almonds, breadcrumbs and suet. Stir in the marmalade (chop the peel if it is very coarse) and the grated rind and juice of the lemons.

Add the sieved flour, salt, nutmeg and cinnamon to the mixture with the sugar. Beat 275 ml of stout with the eggs, then add to the mixture and stir well. The mixture should be beautifully moist but not sloppy. If necessary, add more stout.

This mixture should make 2 puds. Place the mixture in greased basins. For easy removal, it makes good sense to put a little piece of greaseproof paper at the bottom. Cover with buttered greaseproof paper and foil and secure with a double-thick, post-office-type elastic band.

Now for my special tip:
Take a very long piece of heavy duty foil and fold it in 6 lengthwise. This makes a sling which you slip under the pudding basin before suspending it, by means of the sling, in a pan of boiling water. The basin should be three-quarters submerged, but should not touch the bottom of the pan. Once the basin, supported by its sling, is properly positioned in the pan, fold the ends of the foil over the sides of the pan and secure firmly in position with the lid. It is not as complicated as it sounds — and it removes the risk of burning the base of the pudding.

I steam/boil my puddings for 12 hours. The minimum time would be 6 hours for a paler pud. If you have tightly fitting lids there is very little evaporation of water from the pan, but do keep your eye on the water level and replenish with boiling water if necessary.

Store in the freezer.

Fried Christmas Pud with Preserved Figs

This is an excellent way to use left-over Christmas pud — it gives it a completely new guise.

left-over Christmas pud cut into thick slices (allow 1 slice per person)
butter
preserved figs and syrup
brandy butter (see p 7)

Melt a generous knob of butter in a frying pan. Do not allow it to burn. Place slices of Christmas pud in the pan and reduce the heat. You need to heat the pudding through without burning it or making it dry.

Meanwhile, place one fig per slice of pudding plus some of the syrup from the figs in a small pan and heat gently. When the pudding is heated through — and it takes about 10 minutes — serve topped with a spoonful of brandy butter. Add a heated fig and some hot syrup. This melts the brandy butter into the pud and is quite delicious.

Christmas Fritters

about 700 g left-over Christmas pudding
chilled brandy butter (see p 7)
100 g cake flour
pinch of salt
15 ml oil
150 ml water
2 egg whites
fat for deep frying
icing sugar

Divide the pudding into 18 equal pieces and mould each into a ball about the size of a walnut. A small portion of brandy butter can be encased in the centre of the pudding if you like. Chill well.

Place the flour and salt in a food processor. Turn on and pour the oil and water through the chute. Blend until smooth.

Whisk the egg whites until stiff and then fold into the batter. Dip a few balls of pudding at a time into the batter and deep-fry immediately at 190°C until golden and crisp. Drain well. Serve as soon as possible after frying, dusted lightly with icing sugar. Extra brandy butter can be served alongside.

Serves 6.

Cocktail Party Food

(Illustrated on page 28)

Somehow the word 'cocktail' reeks of the thirties. Perhaps the term 'drinks party' is more of this decade.

I do agree that cocktail food can be fiddly to make but if you can persuade your friends to help, you can have a merry party-before-the-party. (Of course, you would then have to help them in return …)

Even Impatient Cooks have to do a bit of mass entertaining at one time or other. If you are really pushed for time, buy lots of **pâtés** from a reliable shop and then proceed to give them your special touch.

First and foremost, banish the soggy toast and the shop-bought savoury biscuit as the base for pâtés. Make my cheese pastry (see p 54). If you are using my pâté recipes, you will find that the Chicken Liver, Taramasalata and Roquefort Cheese ones pipe beautifully.

If you don't know how to pipe, read my quick lesson on page 44. After 15 minutes of practice, anyone should be able to make a reasonable attempt to pipe the occasional rosette.

Pipe whatever pâtés you are going to use on to the bases and garnish with slivers of black olives, green olives, stuffed olives, triangles of cucumber, triangles of red pimento, tiny sprigs of herbs … in fact, anything edible that will enhance the appearance.

Another topping for the cheese pastry bases is smooth cream cheese — the best quality you can find — spiced up with different herbs, black pepper and a little grated lemon rind. Decorate these with cooked, shelled baby prawns.

Good presentation is vital, so find big platters and set your goodies in straight lines of identical canapés across the platters, garnished with sprigs of fresh herbs or interesting sprays of small flowers.

Caviar Balls

Well, sort of caviar ... in fact lumpfish roe caviar. You need smooth cream cheese for this canapé. My favourite is Philadelphia cream cheese because it is not a 'wet' cheese. Cut a large pack into twelve portions. Roll each portion into a ball in your hands. Reserve. Within 2-3 hours of eating, take an egg-cup and put 2-3 teaspoons of caviar into it. Place a ball of cheese on top of the caviar and, with a bouncing movement (and your hand over the top of the egg-cup to stop the cheese ball bouncing out), coat the ball on all sides. Remove with a cocktail stick and place in small paper cups. This is vital as they leak a little and would spoil the appearance of other foods on the same platter. Do half in red caviar and half in black.

Smoked Salmon Canapés

Spread crustless brown bread with softened butter. Top with smoked salmon. Don't attempt to cut into shapes with cutters as the smoked salmon will tear. Cut into triangles with a sharp knife, remembering that all cocktail food should be able to be eaten with one bite. Garnish with triangles of cucumber skin. You do this by taking the skin off the cucumber with a swivel potato peeler and then cutting it into diamonds or triangles.

These little goodies can be made ahead of time and frozen.

Another, easier, version is to roll out a crustless slice of brown bread with a rolling-pin to make it thin. Butter and cover with smoked salmon or smoked trout (and don't be stingy with the butter). Place the open sandwich on a piece of greaseproof paper and roll it up tightly, securing the roll by twisting the paper at either end. Freeze.

Half an hour before serving, remove from the freezer. Remove the paper and slice into 6 rounds.

Anchovy Crescents

Use puff or shortcrust pastry — either home-made or shop-bought.

Roll out the pastry and cut into 5 cm circles. Place 1 canned anchovy (preferably the ones that come with a caper rolled inside) in the middle of the pastry circle. Brush the edges of the pastry with an egg yolk beaten with a little milk. Fold over and seal to form a crescent. Brush with the egg yolk mixture, making a tiny cross in the pastry with the end of a sharp knife. Bake in a preheated oven at 210°C until golden brown.

Bacon and Prune Rolls

Soak some prunes overnight in brandy or cold black tea. Remove the stones. Roll the prunes in a rasher of streaky bacon and anchor with a cocktail stick. Grill until crispy.

Cherry Tomatoes stuffed with Smoked Snoek Pâté

This really is an instant goodie.

Cut the tops off the cherry tomatoes, cutting the opposite end to the one that came off the stalk. With a pair of thin-bladed kitchen scissors, cut inside the tomato and remove the pulp with the end of a teaspoon. Leave to drain, upside down.

Use instant smoked snoek pâté and give it a good stir before either piping or spooning into the tomatoes. Put the tomato cap back on and serve in small paper cups.

Steak Tartare

200 g minced lean sirloin steak
30 ml baby gherkins, chopped finely
15-20 ml capers, chopped finely
30 ml parsley, chopped finely
5 ml Dijon mustard
Tabasco sauce to taste — don't go too mad!
Worcestershire sauce
10 ml brandy
salt and freshly ground black pepper

Mix all the ingredients together. Roll into little balls and serve on pieces of red lettuce. Serve with triangles of toast (yes, in spite of my remarks about cold soggy toast).

Do keep this platter chilled until the last minute. Garnish with sprigs of watercress, slices of hard-boiled egg and slivers of lemon.

Sardine Oblongs

2 x 125 g cans sardines
fresh lemon juice
salt and freshly ground black pepper
bran biscuits
paprika
fresh parsley, chopped
butter

Place the sardines, lemon juice, salt and pepper into a food processor. Use just enough lemon juice to add some zest. Blend until smooth. Spread some of the mixture on lightly buttered biscuits and mark a cross with the paprika and parsley.

Salami Cornets

Use either cottage cheese flavoured with a little grated lemon rind and chopped parsley, or any pâté left over from the other snacks. Roll the salami slices into a cone shape and anchor the base with a cocktail stick. Pipe in your choice of filling.

Celery Snacks

Cut bite-sized pieces of celery. Fill the cavity with cottage cheese. Top with slivers of browned nuts.

Stuffed Grapes

In the old days when I trained at the London Cordon Bleu School we were taught to skin green grapes but to leave the skins on black grapes (otherwise they both look the same). However, don't bother, just leave the skins on both.

It is vital, though, to remove the pips. This is done with the end of a hairgrip or a paperclip that has been slightly bent. You just hook out the pips through the stalk end of the grape.

Mix smooth cottage cheese with some chopped fresh herbs and add a little freshly ground black pepper. Pipe the mixture into the hole in the grape, ending with a rosette of cheese. (If you haven't a piping bag, make one out of a double layer of greaseproof paper cut into a triangle. Roll it into a cone and secure the end.)

Serve **Dips** and **Taramasalata** (p 73) with Toast Melba (p 73) savoury biscuits and sticks of fresh vegetables.

Party Drinks

The original idea came from my friend Shirley who made a slushy sorbet from kiwi fruit juice (shop-bought) mixed with vodka to the ratio of 5:1. Place a spoonful in a wine glass and top with well chilled dry sparkling wine. If you have a proper ice-cream machine you will be able to make a firmer sorbet.

I then experimented with Campari and orange juice blended into a sorbet and served with dry sparkling wine. And apricot juice mixed with apricot brandy and topped with sparkling dry wine.

It certainly made a party to remember!

Remember, you do need slightly larger glasses to prevent spills.

Coconut Crunchies

I have made these biscuits for years and only recently discovered a good substitute for rolled oats. I found a packet of wheat cereal in the cupboard and substituted 100 g wheat cereal in place of the rolled oats and cornflakes. To my great surprise, I found these crunchies were even nicer.

100 g soft brown sugar
75 g desiccated coconut
75 g rolled oats and 25 g cornflakes OR 100 g wheat cereal
125 g butter
15 ml dark, clear honey

Mix together the soft brown sugar, coconut, oats and cornflakes (or wheat cereal). Melt the butter and mix with the honey. Stir into the dry ingredients.

Grease two shallow 18 cm sandwich tins. Spoon the mixture into the two sandwich tins and press down well (the mixture will be fairly dry). Make certain that the mixture is not thin at the edges, otherwise it will burn. Bake in a preheated oven at 170°C for approximately 30 minutes until golden brown.

Cut into slices while hot, but leave them in the tin until they are cold.

Coffee Meringue Gâteau

This dessert was invented by a member of my church, Jean Richards. We have used it often for big church parties, with great success. You don't have to be clever and pipe anything — you just spread the meringue. It's a winner as you make it ahead of time and freeze it.

1 batch of meringue made with 5 egg whites (see p 43)
300 ml cream
icing sugar to taste (start with 45 ml)
5-10 ml instant coffee granules or powder

Line 3 baking trays with baking paper. Take a ruler and mark out with a pencil 3 rectangles measuring approximately 250 mm by 130 mm. Spread the raw meringue over the baking paper to fill the rectangles. Neaten the edges with the blade of a knife. Bake in a preheated oven at 100°C, preferably overnight.

Whip the cream stiffly and stir in the sugar and coffee. You need to taste the bite of the coffee granules — if it still tastes insipid, add some more. (The amount needed really depends on the brand of coffee you use.)

Place one layer of meringue on to a baking sheet. Spread with the cream mixture. Top with a second layer of meringue. Spread with the cream mixture. Top with the third layer of meringue. If you have any cream mixture left over spread it on top. But don't worry if you haven't. Freeze and then cover with cling wrap.

Take the gâteau out of the freezer 45 minutes before serving. To make it look professional, spread a little whipped cream over the top and sides. Don't make it too thick. Sprinkle with chopped nuts or grated chocolate, or decorate with fresh strawberries. Cut into serving pieces when it is still frozen. Use the serrated knife recommended for deep-freeze cutting — if you have one. Otherwise use a bread knife. It cuts into beautifully neat slices. Allow the slices to thaw on individual serving plates.

Serves 8.

Instant Courgettes

This is a method rather than a recipe.

Wash, dry and top and tail any number of courgettes (baby marrows). Grate coarsely by hand or in a food processor. Liberally butter a large frying pan and add the grated courgettes.

Cook over a medium heat until courgettes are heated completely. This should take no longer than a minute or two. Remove from the heat, season with salt and freshly ground black pepper. Stir in a dash of cream (or more, depending on the amount of courgettes cooked), and return to the heat for 1 minute.

Serve immediately.

Couscous

Couscous makes a delicious stuffing for chicken. See Moroccan Chicken (p 14). This is a simple microwave method.

250 ml water
50 ml oil
2,5 ml salt
250 g couscous

Mix the water, oil and salt in a large microwave bowl. Microwave on full power for 3 minutes. The liquid must be boiling. Stir in the couscous. Microwave for 1½-2 minutes. Stir twice during the cooking time. Allow to stand for 5 minutes. It isn't necessary to cover the couscous during cooking.

My Crêpes

Everyone was surprised when I wanted to include crêpes among what are intended to be fairly quick recipes.

However, they can be used in so many fast dishes that I think it is worth while to make a batch and freeze any unused ones. The actual time taken to make them is short. They are easy and when turned into my fastest show-off dessert, Crêpes Suzette, should really suit the Impatient Gourmet!

Crêpe mixture — sufficient for 15 small elegant crêpes

A good crêpe should be thin enough to read through — and the secret is to get the batter to the thinness of pouring cream.

125 g cake flour
pinch of salt
2 jumbo eggs
300 ml milk
15 ml oil

Place the flour and salt in a food processor or liquidiser/blender. Turn on and add the rest of the ingredients through the chute, blending well until the mixture is bubbly and smooth. Keep in a cool place for at least 30 minutes before using. The flour will thicken during this time — and it varies every time. If the mixture appears thicker than pouring cream, just blend in a little extra milk.

Take a small non-stick pan (for preference — although any pan can be seasoned by heating it empty and then rubbing it with a piece of pork fat) and rub with a pad of kitchen towel impregnated with oil. Heat the pan to hot. The secret of a thin crêpe is that a thin layer of the batter must adhere to the pan the *second* that it touches it.

Take a kitchen ladle and half-fill with batter. Take the pan in one hand and pour the mixture from the ladle with the other. Swirl the pan so that the mixture coats all over. The first crêpe is never madly successful as you are judging how much mixture is needed to just coat the pan thinly. Continue cooking until the wet look has left the top of the crêpe. Then, with a small spatula, gently turn the golden crêpe over. Brown the other side and gently slide on to greaseproof paper. Layer each thin pancake with paper to prevent sticking. Wrap in foil and store either in fridge or freezer.

To turn these crêpes into that classic, **Crêpes Suzette**, make the fragrant sauce by mixing the following in a processor or liquidiser/blender:

200 g butter
100 g castor sugar
grated rind and juice of 1 big juicy orange
grated rind and juice of 1 juicy lemon
60 ml Cointreau (in impoverished times I have used sherry)

The mixture comes out looking a curdled mess but don't worry. Take a big generous spoonful and place it in a large frying pan. When it is bubbling, take a crêpe by the edges and dip it into the mixture. Fold it in half, with the coated surface to the inside. Turn it with spatulas, folding it in half again and push it neatly to one side. Continue until the pan is full. If necessary add a little more of the buttery mixture.

Take approximately 10-15 ml of brandy and pour over. Wait just a few seconds and then ignite, shaking well so that the flames burn away the fat, leaving a glorious flavour. Have warmed plates ready. Slip the folded crêpes (allow 2 per person) on to the plates and insist that they are eaten immediately. Continue until the crêpes and butter are finished. Allow for second helpings.

Crêpes make a wonderful stretcher of left-overs. Try filling them with Bolognese sauce and topping with grated cheese. Or fill with left-over slivers of ham mixed with lightly fried mushroom slivers and a cup of white sauce. Prawn Salpicon mixture (see p 58) rolled in crêpes makes an elegant starter.

Or layer like a cake with the following mixture:

1 x 385 g can apples
45 ml soft brown sugar
5 ml ground cinnamon
5 ml ground nutmeg
grated rind and juice of 1 lemon
grated rind and juice of 1 orange
30 g butter

Mix the apples, sugar, cinnamon, nutmeg and rinds and juice of orange and lemon together in a microwave dish. Cover with cling wrap and microwave on full power for 4-5 minutes. Add the butter, beating well until it melts.

Place one crêpe on a microwave plate and top it with some of the apple mixture. Continue to alternate crêpes with mixture until all the mixture has been used. Sprinkle additional brown sugar over the top. Microwave on full power for $1^1/_2$ minutes.

Crispy Coatings

Battered fish

125 g flour
pinch of salt
2 eggs
15 ml oil
280 ml milk

Sift the flour with the salt. Beat in 1 whole egg and 1 yolk with the milk — it's easy in a food processor. Add the oil. Beat until bubbly. Leave to stand for 30 minutes.

When ready to use, whisk the remaining egg white and fold it into the mixture. Dip the fish into the batter and fry immediately.

A quick fish coating

Wipe the fish and then dip in lightly seasoned flour. Beat a jumbo egg with salt and pepper and 15 ml chopped parsley. Dip the fish into this batter and then fry.

When coating with breadcrumbs, first coat with seasoned flour. Secondly, coat with beaten egg and then dip into breadcrumbs. It's easiest if you have 3 plates and use spatulas — otherwise you can get very messy.

Croques Monsieur

What a snack! Children love it as a 'high tea'. Fattening and gorgeous.

125 g Cheddar cheese
125 ml cream
salt and pepper
8 thin slices white bread (not too fresh)
4 thin slices ham
75 g butter
15 ml butter
15 ml flour
150 ml milk

Grate the cheese and reserve 30 ml. Mix the rest of the cheese with enough cream to make a thick paste. Save about 15-25 ml of the cream for the sauce. Season with a little salt and pepper. Cut the crusts off the bread and spread each slice with the cheese mixture. Put one slice of ham between two cheese covered slices. Press together (cheese sides inwards) and cut in half diagonally. Heat 75 g butter in a frying pan until hot. *Do not burn.* Fry the sandwiches on both sides until crisp and golden, adding a little more butter if necessary. Drain on paper towel. Arrange on a hot dish and keep warm.

To make the sauce melt the 15 ml butter, add the flour and 'mellow' for a minute or two. Blend in the milk, beating well to avoid lumps. A small whisk makes a smooth sauce easily. Season. Add the remaining cheese. Stir over a gentle heat until the cheese has melted. Stir in the cream, pour over the sandwiches, and serve immediately.

D

Delectable Dessert

This recipe is a must! It is irresistible and terribly rich. Serve it with my Special Fruit Salad (p 36).

Even if you hate to cook, there must be times when it's not so bad. Chop the chocolate, dates and nuts then. They will store beautifully in the freezer, ready to be dragged out when you want to indulge.

250 g pecans or walnuts
250 g dark chocolate
250 g dates
6 egg whites
125 g castor sugar

to decorate:
whipped cream, chocolate curls (if you have the time) and a can of drained mandarin oranges

The secret of making this recipe relatively painless is to chop the nuts, chocolate and dates together in the food processor using the metal blade. If you try to do the dates separately, they will clog the blade and almost burn out the motor. So break the chocolate coarsely, whilst it is still in the packet, by thumping it against the counter. Cut the dates into big pieces. Then drop all three ingredients through the chute as the machine is going. You need them to be coarsely chopped, not ground into a fine powder.

Whip the egg whites in an electric mixer until they form peaks. Take care to check first that the bowl and whisk are absolutely free from grease and liquid. Also make certain that the egg whites are at room temperature to get maximum bulk. Add the sugar, a little at a time. Beat until the sugar has been absorbed and the mixture is very stiff. You should be able to turn the bowl upside down without losing any of the mixture. (Maybe you had better not try it!) It really is easy and doesn't take more than 5 minutes.

Fold the egg whites into the nut/chocolate/date mixture and then spoon it into a cake tin (23 cm) which has been lined with oiled baking paper. This is the bit that I hate doing. It makes life easier if the tin has a removable bottom. Cook in a preheated oven at 180°C for 45 minutes. Turn the oven off. Leave the door slightly open and leave the dessert to cool in the oven.

You can make this dessert the day before it is needed and store it in the fridge in the baking tin.

Turn out on to a serving plate, top with whipped cream, chocolate curls (made by taking a swivel potato peeler down the side of a bar of dark chocolate which has been warmed in the hand) and mandarin segments.

Serves 8 generously.

Dressings

Parsley and Walnut Dressing

This is a delicious dressing to serve over warm cooked prawns, or with a watercress salad.

250 ml fresh parsley
1 clove garlic, crushed
80 ml olive oil
2,5 ml salt
15 ml lemon juice
125 ml walnuts

Put the parsley, garlic and half the oil in a food processor. Process for 30 seconds.

Scrape the sides of the machine and continue processing, adding all the remaining ingredients, except the walnuts. Add the walnuts at the last minute as they need to be only lightly chopped.

Check the seasoning — the chances are that it will need a little extra salt.

Opposite: Chilli con Carne
Overleaf: (left) Cocktail Party Food and
(right) Fish Oriental
Page 30: Special Fruit Salad with Champagne Sauce
Prepared with choice ingredients from Woolworths food markets

Salad Dressing

125 ml wine vinegar
60 ml grated Parmesan cheese
15 ml sugar
10 ml salt
5 ml celery salt
2,5 ml freshly ground black pepper
2,5 ml dry mustard
generous sprinkling of paprika
2 cloves garlic, crushed
350 ml salad oil

Mix all the ingredients together, except the oil. Whisk well until dissolved. Gradually add the oil and stir for 2-3 minutes.

Sherry Dressing

A versatile dressing that is good with almost any salad.

1 jumbo egg
2,5 ml sugar
2,5 ml salt
freshly ground black pepper
1 small clove garlic, crushed
250 ml oil
75 ml wine vinegar
50 ml dry sherry

Place the egg in a food processor or liquidiser / blender and blend. Add the sugar, salt, black pepper and garlic. Gradually add the oil, then the vinegar and sherry. Allow to stand for 2 hours before use.

Sweet-Pepper Dressing

Best made the day before required to allow the pimento flavour to permeate the dressing. Especially good with Sunflower Tomatoes (p 74).

250 ml oil
125 ml wine vinegar
5 ml salt
5 ml dry mustard
10 ml castor sugar
225 g canned or bottled pimentos (red peppers), drained and chopped

Place all the ingredients together in a jar with a screw-top lid. Shake vigorously until well mixed. Chill and use as required.

Tomato and Yoghurt Salad Dressing

A delicious dressing to serve with red-leaf lettuce and chopped avocado.

60 ml oil
5 ml salt
5 ml castor sugar
30 ml wine vinegar
300 ml tomato juice
175 ml thick natural yoghurt
6 spring onions, chopped
30 ml horseradish sauce
freshly ground black pepper

Place the oil, salt, sugar, vinegar and tomato juice in a food processor or liquidiser / blender and blend. Add the yoghurt, spring onions, horseradish and pepper. Blend.

E

Egg Mousse with Devilled Prawns

When you read the list of ingredients, you might be inclined to pass over this recipe. Don't! It tastes wonderful and is so easy to make. I often have luncheon parties when I only serve pâtés, terrines and mousses — and this one is always a winner. Guests — like my friend Derek Chapman — keep asking for it.

6 eggs, hard-boiled
250 ml thick mayonnaise
20 ml gelatine
75 ml chicken stock
15 ml anchovy essence or sauce (it goes under the brand name of Burgess)
125 ml cream
salt and pepper
watercress to garnish

Devilled mixture
175 ml tomato sauce
10 ml Worcestershire sauce
3 drops Tabasco sauce
225 g prawns, cooked and shelled

Chop the eggs. It's fine to do it in the food processor as long as you use the pulse button for just a few seconds — otherwise you end up with egg paste. Add the mayonnaise.

Meanwhile, place 45 ml of cold chicken stock in a small ramekin and shake the measured gelatine over the surface. Leave for 1 minute for the mixture to turn into a solid 'cake'. Place in the microwave for about 30 seconds until the mixture is translucent but has not boiled over. (If you haven't got a microwave, heat the gelatine mixture over a very low heat on top of the stove.)

Leave to stand for 1 minute and then add through the chute of the processor together with the remaining cold stock and anchovy essence. Whip the cream until thickening, season, and then fold into the egg mixture. Take care not to oversalt.

Pour into a serving bowl. Cover with cling wrap and chill in the fridge for 3 hours.

Meanwhile make the sauce by mixing together the tomato sauce, Worcestershire sauce, Tabasco and prawns. Take care when choosing the prawns. Some cooked prawns taste like pieces of ironing blanket.

When the mousse is firm, spoon the devilled mixture on top and decorate with watercress. Serve with Toast Melba (p 73).

Serves 8 as a starter.

Framed Eggs

A breakfast special.

Remove the centre from a slice of bread with a pastry cutter. Brown the bread on both sides in hot bacon fat (or butter) in a frying pan. Break an egg in the hole in the centre and fry till set.

Don't waste the centres of the bread slices. Turn them into breadcrumbs (in the food processor) and store in the freezer until needed to coat fish or make stuffing for poultry.

Poached Eggs

The microwave way.

For 2 poached eggs, I use a small dish which is 180 mm by 110 mm. The actual timing will depend on the type of dish (and how it allows the microwaves through into the food) as well as on the performance of the microwave oven.

Put boiling water from the kettle (it speeds up the cooking time) into a small dish. Add 10 ml lemon juice or vinegar. Microwave for 1 minute — or a little longer — until the water is bubbling. Add the eggs. Cover with cling wrap and microwave on full power for about 1 minute and 8 seconds. Allow to stand.

Serve on hot buttered toast.

The final timing for eggs just the way you like them should be easily established — with maybe just one or two mishaps. But if you undercook, you can just give additional 10-second blasts until you get it perfect every time.

Scotch Surprise Eggs

Great as a picnic item.

Perfect hard-boiled eggs are not easy. Have the eggs at room temperature. Carefully place in boiling water and roll each egg to set the yolk in the middle. Simmer for 10 minutes. Break the shells and cool under cold running water. With the back of the bowl of a spoon, rap each shell all over to break it. Roll the egg on the counter to loosen the shell and gently ease off with the aid of a teaspoon. It is less laborious than it sounds.

500 g potatoes, peeled weight
60 g butter
125 g cheese, grated
30 ml garlic chives, chopped
salt and freshly ground black pepper
4 jumbo eggs, hard-boiled and peeled
1 jumbo egg, beaten
100 g fresh brown breadcrumbs
oil

Boil the potatoes until tender. Mash and push through a sieve or ricer. (You don't have to do this, but it does make it extra special.)

Mix the potato with the butter, cheese, garlic chives and seasoning. Divide the mixture into 4 portions and place on a lightly floured board. Place one peeled hard-boiled egg in the middle of each pile of potato. Mould the potato round the egg, covering it completely and moulding the potato into the shape of the egg. Roll gently in the beaten egg and then in the breadcrumbs. Chill in the fridge to firm. Deep-fry in hot oil until golden and crisp.

Scrambled Eggs

My daughter Sarah makes the most delicious, creamy, flavourful scrambled eggs. The secret is in the timing. Remember, eggs cook on — so turn the stove off when the mixture is still fairly wet.

eggs (use 6 eggs for 4 people)
salt and white pepper (black pepper looks awful)
butter
chopped chives or slivers of smoked salmon (if you feel like indulging)

Beat the eggs with the salt and pepper. Melt a generous knob of butter in a pan but do not let it burn. Add the eggs and allow to settle. Using a wooden spoon, stir gently from the bottom. Add the chives or salmon. Continue stirring until the eggs are cooked but the mixture is still slightly wet. Remove from the stove and get an assembly job done, putting bacon, mushrooms, sausages ... whatever, on to hot plates. Give the eggs a final stir and if they still look a little wet, give them another minute on the stove.

Serve immediately.

F

Fish Oriental

(Illustrated on page 29)

1-2 nuggets of loin of kingklip per person
300 ml milk
30 g butter
30 g flour
salt and pepper to taste
1 x 425 g can litchis
1 x 310 g can mandarins
chopped parsley

Place the fish in a buttered casserole. Pour the milk over the fish and season. Cover loosely with buttered paper. Cook in a preheated oven at 180°C for 20-25 minutes. Drain off the liquid and make up to 300 ml with the juice from the canned fruit.

Make a white sauce by melting the butter in a pan and stirring in the flour. 'Mellow' for a minute or two before adding the liquid, a little at a time, beating well. Once all the liquid has been added, continue cooking until the sauce has thickened. It should have a creamy consistency. If necessary, add a little more fruit juice. Adjust the seasoning. Add about 2 litchis and 3 mandarins per piece of fish to the sauce. Pour over the fish.

Sprinkle with chopped parsley before serving.

Fish Parcels

Nice and easy to serve as each person has an individual parcel.

cutlets of kingklip, hake or any line fish
buttered rectangles of foil for each cutlet
onion slices
sprigs of fresh herbs, such as dill
lemon slices
salt and freshly ground black pepper
white wine, if available — otherwise a little lemon juice
small bay leaves
knobs of butter

Place each cutlet of fish on a piece of buttered foil. Top with two slices of onion, a sprig of herb, 1 slice of lemon, a sprinkling of salt and pepper. Pour over a sprinkling of wine or lemon juice. Place 1 small bay leaf on top with a knob of butter.

Secure the parcels, making sure they are sealed tent-like rather than like a tight bandage. Place on a baking sheet and bake in a preheated oven at 180°C. Cooking time will depend on the thickness of the fish but try 20 minutes to start with. The parcels can easily be resealed and returned to the oven, but take care not to overcook.

Fish Platter

This makes a spectacular and easy starter for a large dinner party.

This is a method rather than a recipe. The most important thing is to have a large, attractive platter. Collect together as large a variety as possible of canned, smoked shellfish and other fish. My suggestions would be:

smoked oysters
smoked mussels
smoked clams
smoked trout
smoked eel
smoked salmon (if you are feeling extravagant)
smoked snoek
smoked herring
smoked kippers
canned mussels in their shells
and, in fact, anything interesting you see in your favourite store.

Drain all the canned ingredients. Arrange the seafood attractively on a large platter, decorated with slices of lemon and sprigs of fresh herbs, such as dill.

Serve with thinly sliced brown bread and butter and two dishes of mayonnaise. To one dish of mayonnaise add very finely chopped watercress leaves, tarragon and parsley sprigs. To the other dish, add some tomato ketchup, cream, lemon juice, a dash of Worcestershire sauce and a few drops of Tabasco sauce. As an alternative, serve a dish of horseradish sauce.

The number of servings will depend on how many smoked goodies you have bought.

Flaming Fish

This is a method rather than a recipe. This delightful way of cooking fish started in the Mediterranean. The fish is cooked in a jacket of herbs.

First braai the whole fish, having just sprinkled it with some black pepper and lemon juice. Then transfer it to a braaipan filled with coarse salt which has been covered with herbs. Rosemary, fennel, dill, parsley or thyme can be used.

Place the fish on top of the herbs and then pour about 90 ml of warmed brandy over the top. Set light to the brandy and the burning herbs will give the fish a subtle flavour which most people find irresistible. Fish fillets can also be cooked by this method.

The brandy will flame quickly and efficiently if it has been carefully warmed first.

Florentinas

A tiny version of Florentines. These are great as they can be served for tea — or as an emergency dessert.

100 g butter
125 g castor sugar
125 g chopped walnuts or almonds
30 g chopped sultanas
50 g chopped glacé cherries
30 g candied peel
15 ml whipped cream
30 ml flour
125 g dark chocolate

Melt the butter, add the sugar and cook until the sugar is dissolved. Boil for one minute. Add all the other ingredients except the chocolate. Mix well. Put in tiny well-spaced spoonfuls on baking sheet lined with baking paper and bake at 180°C until golden. Remove and cool. Loosen with a palette knife after 1 minute.

Melt the chocolate (see p 17) and then spread over the Florentinas. With a fork scratch marks on the chocolate surface.

Should make at least 20.

Fruit Brie

Fruit Brie really has a Christmassy look. This is a method rather than a recipe.

big, seeded or seedless raisins
big juicy sultanas
a few currants
port
whole Brie

Soak the fruit in port for 2 days. Keep a whole Brie out of the fridge for about 8 hours — or until it is runny. Scoop the cheese out of the shell and mix with the macerated fruit. Place back in the shell. Serve with Toast Melba (see p 73).

Fruit Crumble

This is a very quick, homely dessert — and the food processor makes it even quicker. Any fruit can be used but if you are in a tearing rush, use canned apples.

1 x 385 g can apples
75 ml brown sugar
30 ml lemon juice
5 ml ground cinnamon
5 ml ground nutmeg
tiny pinch ground cloves
125 g flour
pinch of salt
60 ml castor sugar
60 ml cold butter

Mix the canned apples with the brown sugar, lemon juice, cinnamon, nutmeg and cloves. Place in a shallow casserole.

Put the flour, salt and castor sugar in the processor, using the metal blade, and turn on. Add the butter, in pieces, through the chute and mix until it resembles breadcrumbs. Spread on top of the apple mixture.

If you have a very sweet tooth, sprinkle some sugar over the top. Bake in a preheated oven at 180°C for approximately 35 minutes or until golden.

It's even nicer with blueberries.

Just wash a punnet of blueberries and place in a microwave dish with a couple of spoonfuls of water and sugar. Cover with cling wrap and cook on full power for 4 minutes. Check if cooked sufficiently and taste for sweetness. Hopefully the dish you have used can be transferred to the oven. Spread the topping over the blueberries and bake as above.

Serve hot with thick cream.

Serves 4.

Special Fruit Salad

(Illustrated on page 30)

seasonal fresh fruits to include:
apples
pears
oranges
melon
pineapple
strawberries
cherries
black grapes
green grapes
bananas
mangoes
but not papaw, although you can include papino

lots of lemon juice
icing sugar
Cointreau or any orange-based liqueur

Peel green apples and steep in lemon juice, after coring and cutting into neat slices. Leave the skin on red apples. It looks more attractive. Core and slice and steep in lemon juice to prevent discolouring. Prepare the rest of the fruit by cutting into slices. Strawberries can either be left whole or cut in half. Only steep fruit that is likely to discolour. You can use the same juice again.

Drain the fruit that has been steeped very well. Take a tall container. A big flower vase would be fine. Place one layer of fruit on the bottom. Sift icing sugar over that fruit. Continue with another layer of fruit, sift with icing sugar, and so on. Finish with a layer of icing sugar and then pour on 30 ml Cointreau for each 450 g fruit. Cover and refrigerate for about 5 hours. The liqueur drips through the sugar taking the natural fruit juices with it.

Pour the fruit salad into the serving bowl just before serving — the smell is mouth-watering. Garnish with sprigs of mint or borage.

Serve with cream, ice-cream, or my Champagne Sauce (see p 63).

Winter Fruit Salad with Cottage Cheese

Labour time: 5 minutes!

800 g mixture of dried fruits (I use dried peaches, apricots, raisins, sultanas, prunes and dried figs)
1 litre pure orange juice
250 ml castor sugar
250 ml whisky
smooth cottage cheese
brown sugar

Put the fruit into a casserole. Meanwhile mix the juice and castor sugar together in a pan and bring to the boil. Simmer until all the sugar has dissolved. Add the whisky. Pour over the fruit and cover tightly.

Cook in a preheated oven at 120°C for 4 hours — or until the fruit has absorbed most of the liquid.

This fruit salad keeps beautifully. Serve with scoops of cottage cheese topped with brown sugar.

Serves 6-8.

Grilled Lamb Cutlets with Gooseberry and Apple Sauce

This is an 18th-century dish — with a new look. Simple but very pleasant.

8-12 lamb cutlets or chops
1 x 400 g can Cape gooseberries
60 g butter
3 apples, peeled, cored and sliced
30 ml soft brown sugar
salt and freshly ground black pepper
ground nutmeg

Grill or bake the lamb cutlets or chops following your usual method.

Meanwhile make the sauce. Drain the gooseberries and purée two-thirds of them with all the juice. Reserve the other gooseberries for garnishing. Melt the butter in a pan and sauté the apple slices until golden and soft. Add the sugar and cook until dissolved. Add the puréed gooseberries. Stir. Season well, adding a slight sprinkling of nutmeg. Add the whole gooseberries and heat through.

Serve alongside the crispy, golden chops.

Serves 4-6.

Ham and Pineapple Chicken Patties

Seems lengthy, but it really isn't! It makes an interesting, slightly different family supper.

8 chicken thighs
knob of butter
1 onion, chopped
1 clove of garlic
75 ml rolled oats
125 g ham
1 x 440 g can crushed pineapple
15 ml parsley
2 eggs
flour
75 ml milk
250 ml breadcrumbs
30 ml sesame seeds (optional)
oil

Remove the skin from the chicken and chop the chicken flesh finely in a food processor. Don't turn it into a pulp. Alternatively, you can just chop finely by hand.

Melt the butter in a frying pan and add the chopped onion and crushed garlic, taking care not to burn the garlic as this will impart a bitter taste. Remove from the heat. Stir in the chopped chicken, oats, chopped ham, well-drained crushed pineapple, chopped parsley and one egg. Mix well, and then divide the mixture into 8 and shape into patties.

Toss the patties in flour, then dip in a mixture of the remaining egg, lightly beaten with the milk. Combine the breadcrumbs and sesame seeds and dip the chicken patties in the mixture.

Shallow fry in hot oil over a medium heat until golden brown and cooked. This will take about 6 minutes per side.

Serves 4.

Hot Fudge Sundae

1 x 100 g Mars Bar or Bar One
30 ml milk
slurp of cream
slurp of brandy

Chop up the chocolate bar and place it with the milk in a dish and microwave, covered, for 3 minutes on high, stirring twice. Add the cream and the brandy. Stir well.

Serve over ice-cream or pears.

Enough for 4 servings.

Camembert Ice-Cream

This recipe comes from the 1930s and was popular with the English Upper-Crusties, but it isn't particularly cheap to make.

1 large whole Camembert, soft and mature but not overripe
125 ml thick cream
125 ml whipping cream
cayenne pepper
salt

Mash up the cheese with the two creams. This can be done very successfully in a food processor or liquidiser/blender. Season well with cayenne pepper and salt.

Freeze until just firm but not hard. There is no need to stir the mixture.

Traditionally, this is served in a glass bowl sitting on a bed of crushed ice.

Serves 6.

Ann's Easy Ice-Cream

A very basic ice-cream for children.

1 x 397 g can condensed milk
500 ml evaporated milk

Mix the condensed milk and evaporated milk together. Pour into ice trays. Freeze until almost set.

Remove from the freezer and beat well. For vanilla ice-cream, add 2,5 ml vanilla essence and mix well. Refreeze.

Jacket Baked Onions

Onions baked in their jackets impart a very special flavour to savour!

4 onions
30 g butter
50 ml Parmesan cheese
15 ml chopped parsley
5 ml sugar
salt and pepper

Cut the tops off the onions and scoop out the centres carefully. Chop finely. Melt the butter. Combine with the chopped onion, cheese, parsley, sugar and seasoning. Spoon back into the onions.

Place in a greased ovenproof dish. Bake at 160°C for approximately one hour or until tender.

This can be served as a vegetarian dish, in which case it will serve 2. Alternatively, try serving it with a plain roast such as lamb or beef.

Quickie Kassler Chops

For each Kassler chop, allow

15 ml dark brown sugar
5 ml soy sauce
5 ml wine vinegar

As you come through the door, set the oven to 220°C.

Mix the sugar, soy sauce and vinegar together to a sort of paste. Spread it over the top of the Kassler chops.

You can now take your coat off!

Place the chops in the oven and bake for approximately 18-22 minutes, depending on the thickness of the chops. Turn on the grill and grill lightly until crisp and bubbling.

Meanwhile scrub some potatoes and microwave them between 2 pieces of paper towel. In my microwave 2 potatoes take about 9-10 minutes. Serve with home-made soured cream mixed with either the chopped green tops of spring onions or chopped garlic chives. A green salad makes a good taste match.

To make soured cream:
Mix a good quality fresh cream with fresh lemon juice to the ratio of 250 ml cream : 45 ml lemon juice.

Kedgeree

Originated with the Brits in India and was a very popular dish in Victorian times. Any fish can be used. Superb not only for breakfast or brunch but also as a supper or light luncheon dish. It can be made the day before and reheated.

450 g smoked haddock, cooked and flaked
60 g butter
1 onion, chopped
5 ml curry powder
175 g uncooked rice
3 hard-boiled eggs, sliced or chopped
15 ml anchovy sauce or essence (optional)
75 ml cream
30 ml parsley, chopped

The easiest way to cook the haddock is in the microwave. Place it in a microwave dish with 250 ml milk and a slice of onion. Cover with cling wrap, pierced twice. Cooking time will depend on the thickness of the fish — try 7 minutes on full power and then check. Do not overcook the fish. Reserve the liquid in which the haddock has been cooked.

Melt the butter in a pan and sauté the onion for a minute or so. Add the curry powder and stir well. Cook for a further minute. Add the uncooked rice, stirring well. Add 600 ml haddock stock — if you haven't enough, add a little milk. Cook steadily until the rice is done, watching to see if more milk is required. The liquid must be totally absorbed by the rice.

Add the fish, eggs, anchovy sauce, cream and parsley. Check the seasoning. Heat through and then spoon into a hot serving dish. Garnish with parsley and lemon wedges.

Serves 4.

Anchovy sauce or essence is available in the sauce section of some supermarkets. It does make a difference, as it brings out the true flavour of the fish.

Devilled Kidneys

This makes a delicious breakfast or supper dish.

8 lamb kidneys
15 ml dry mustard
10 ml Worcestershire sauce
60 g butter
salt and freshly ground black pepper

Skin the membrane from the kidneys. Cut in half and remove the core with scissors. Mix the mustard with the Worcestershire sauce.

Melt the butter in a pan and add the kidneys, quickly browning them on all sides. Reduce the heat, cover the pan and cook gently for 5 minutes. Season and add the mustard mixture. Stir well and cook gently for 2 minutes.

Sufficient for 4 breakfast portions.

Kingklip Curry

Try making your own curry mixture. It makes such a difference. Blend cardamom seeds, crushed cinnamon, cloves, cumin seeds, coriander seeds and peppercorns in an electric grinder (make certain you air it well before grinding your next batch of coffee!)

500 g kingklip fillets (yes, you can use hake)
seasoned flour
60 ml butter
30 ml oil
2 onions, finely chopped
15 ml curry powder
30 ml flour
375 ml water
1 carrot, finely sliced
2 sticks table celery, finely sliced
1 apple, peeled, cored and sliced
2 cloves garlic, crushed
125 g tomatoes (canned are fine)
15 ml rich fruity chutney

Cube the fish and toss it in seasoned flour. Heat 30 ml butter and 15 ml oil in a pan and sauté the onions until soft but not brown. Stir in the curry powder and flour and 'mellow' for a minute or two. Add 125 ml water, beating well to avoid lumps. Add 2 further 125 ml of water, stirring well between additions. Add the carrot, celery, apple, garlic and tomatoes. Simmer gently, uncovered, for 30 minutes.

Heat the remaining 30 ml butter and 15 ml oil in a separate pan and brown the fish. Remove from the pan. Add to the sauce together with the chutney and cook gently for 5 minutes. Serve with rice.

Serves 4.

Lemon Meringue Pie, with a Difference

The lemon filling can be cooked in the microwave. I also recommend that you make it earlier so that it can cool. The pastry and the meringue seem much happier without having made contact with a hot lemon sauce. It also means that you can make the pastry shell and the filling before a party. Just whip up the meringue before calling your guests to the table for the first course — the meringue really only takes about $3^1/_2$ minutes to make. It might sound tedious but it's worth the effort. The microwave speeds things up — as does shop-bought pastry.

1 shortcrust pastry shell (baked until golden)
40 g cornflour
350 ml cold water
150-225 g sugar (depending on how sweet a tooth you have)
pinch of salt
grated rind of 1 large lemon
100 ml lemon juice
4 egg yolks
knob of butter
4 egg whites
120 g granulated sugar
120 g icing sugar
little extra sugar for dredging

Make the filling by mixing the cornflour with a little of the 350 ml cold water. Then beat in the rest of the water with the sugar and salt. Place in a microwave oven on full power until boiling and thick — beating well about every other minute. In my microwave it takes 6 minutes. Beat in the lemon rind and juice. Now beat in the egg yolks and return to the microwave.

Remember, microwaves do vary, so take care — otherwise the egg yolks will curdle. Do not move from the microwave but stand there, whisk in hand. Microwave for 1 minute on full power. Whisk like mad. Return to the microwave for 1-minute blasts until the egg yolks have 'cooked in' and thickened the lemon sauce. Beat in the butter.

This really is easy. The microwave is ideal for egg-thickened sauces. Allow to cool — first tasting to see if you have the right sugar balance. If not, add some more now. But remember that the meringue topping is sweet.

Pour the cold filling into the pastry shell.

Make the meringue by beating the egg whites until they form peaks. Add the granulated sugar, a little at a time, beating on maximum power until the mixture is thick, thick, thick ... In fact, it should be so thick that you can turn the bowl upside down without losing any of the mixture. Fold in the sifted icing sugar with a large metal spoon using a figure-of-eight movement with the wrist. This ensures that the sugar is mixed in without knocking out the air already incorporated in the meringue. It really is easy — try it by twisting the metal spoon in the air first. Having a really large spoon helps too.

Spoon or pipe the meringue over the lemon filling, taking care to seal the edges. This prevents the lemon mixture bubbling out in the oven. If you have spooned (rather than piped) the mixture on to the lemon filling, take the back of the bowl of a large spoon and pull it against the meringue. As you pull it away, the meringue will form nice peaks. Dredge with a little additional sifted icing sugar and bake in a preheated oven at 150°C for about 30 minutes.

Serves 6.

Liver and Onion Bake

This is a method rather than a recipe.

Take a baking tin and rub it with oil. Put in a thick layer of *thinly* sliced onions. (If you haven't got a food processor, borrow one!) Season with salt and freshly ground black pepper.

Cover the onions with a thick layer of *thinly* sliced liver. If you chill the liver in the freezer for 30 minutes you will find that it is much easier to slice. Season again and then cover the liver with a thick layer of *thinly* sliced potatoes (use the processor again for speed).

Flick some melted butter (done in 45 seconds in the microwave) over the top and cover with foil. Bake in a preheated oven at 180°C for about 35 minutes and then remove the foil. Turn up the heat to 200°C to crisp and brown the potatoes. I sometimes brown them under the grill, having first made sure that they are completely cooked.

M

Mangetout and Artichokes with Blue Cheese Dressing

Mangetout are sometimes known as snow peas. Artichokes are eaten by pulling the leaves and sucking the thick base part. They are delicious. When all the leaves are removed eat the fleshy heart at the bottom.

Cook the mangetout in boiling salted water for approximately 3 minutes. Drain and refresh in cold water. Cook the artichokes in boiling salted water until one of the leaves pulls out easily (approximately 40 minutes). Drain well. (Out of season, canned artichoke hearts can be substituted.)

Arrange on individual serving dishes, giving each person an artichoke garnished with six mangetout.

Make a dressing by:

Placing 1 jumbo egg, 2,5 ml salt, and 5 ml grainy French mustard in a food processor. Blend for 2 minutes. Add 125 ml oil and a little crumbled blue cheese through the chute. Finish with 20 ml fresh lemon juice. Pour over the artichoke so that the dressing drains down inside and over the mangetout. Chill for 30 minutes before serving.

Flaming Mangoes

Getting the stone out of fresh mangoes is not the easiest job in life. In theory, you cut through the mango from the north pole to the south, right through to the stone and then twist firmly. The mango should separate into 2 halves. You then remove the stone by easing it out with a grapefruit knife. It's easier to use canned ones!

60 ml butter
60 ml sugar
2 lemons
2 oranges
100 ml Cointreau
8 mango halves (either canned or fresh)
100 ml cane

Melt the butter in a frying pan. Add the sugar and stir until dissolved. Thinly pare the outer skin of the lemons and oranges (a swivel potato peeler makes it easy). Add to the frying pan. Add the Cointreau and flame the mixture, shaking the pan well.

Add the juice of the lemons and oranges (which should be approximately 275 ml combined) and cook until the mixture is just turning brown.

Add the mangoes and the cane and flame again.

Serves 4.

Mayonnaise

(Illustrated on page 47)

Please bother! It's only going to take you approximately 6 minutes with a good mixer. It will last for weeks in the refrigerator and makes a gourmet feast out of slivers of left-over chicken with lettuce and fresh brown bread. It makes such a difference in savoury mousses ... in fact, everything tastes nicer.

Watchpoints:

- *Do not* use refrigerator-cold ingredients.
- *Do* beat egg yolks for several minutes until very thick.
- The amount of wine vinegar or lemon juice needed depends on the size of the egg yolks. Start with 30 ml. If the mixture needs to be slightly thinned, add more wine vinegar or lemon juice slowly and a little at a time.

5 jumbo egg yolks at room temperature
5 ml salt
5 ml pepper
5 ml sugar
5 ml dry mustard
500 ml oil at room temperature
wine vinegar or lemon juice

The secret of mayonnaise is to beat the yolks until very, very thick. I am stressing this as it minimises the risk of curdling. Go away and make a telephone call! Add the salt, pepper, sugar and mustard to the beaten egg yolks. Start to add the oil in a very thin stream, beating all the time. When the mixture seems very thick, add 30 ml wine vinegar or lemon juice. Slowly add the rest of the oil. You might need to add a little more vinegar or lemon juice.

You should end up with a large bowl of thick mayonnaise. Adjust the seasoning to taste. It always needs some additional salt and pepper.

Spiced Melon

30 ml butter
30 ml onion, finely chopped
5 ml curry powder
pinch of ground ginger (fresh — not a jar that has been lurking for years)
4 slices melon

Heat the butter in a pan and sauté the onion until soft but not brown. Add the curry powder and ginger and 'mellow' for a minute or two. Dry the slices of melon and add to the pan, sautéing for a minute or two on each side.

Serves 4, as a delicious accompaniment to grilled lamb chops.

My Never-Fail Meringues

(Illustrated on page 48)

Be bothered as, with practice, you can make a beautiful meringue nest in 10 minutes from start to finish.

Just follow the rules ... to the letter!

- Do not use fresh eggs. They should be at least 10 days old. However, unless you have your own chickens, you need not worry. It's unlikely that the eggs would be younger than 10 days.
- Make certain that the egg whites are at room temperature to get maximum whipped bulk.
- Make certain that you haven't got the smallest speck of yolk in the whites. If you have, remove it with the rough edge of a broken egg-shell.
- Make certain that the bowl and the whisk are free from grease — otherwise the egg whites won't whisk properly.
- Line the baking trays with baking paper for easy removal.
- Don't make meringues in a damp atmosphere. It's often better to make them late at night when no other cooking is taking place.
- If you live in humid conditions, freeze meringues if you are not using them immediately. As long as you have a bone-dry storage area, meringues keep perfectly for ages. In England I kept a store of meringues in an open cardboard box next to the hot water tank.
- Have patience. You mustn't rush the adding of the sugar.
- Always sift the icing sugar — otherwise you could get little cloggy lumps.

For a large meringue nest, use

5 jumbo egg whites (use the yolks for mayonnaise)
150 g castor sugar
150 g sifted icing sugar

Beat the egg whites until they are beginning to form peaks. Continue beating on maximum, adding the castor sugar a little at a time until it has all been added. Continue beating until the mixture is very thick. It should be thick enough for the bowl to be turned upside down without losing a speck of meringue.

Add the sifted icing sugar and fold in with a large metal spoon, turning the spoon in a figure-of-eight movement. This ensures that you mix from the bottom, incorporating the icing sugar without knocking out the lightness from the whisked egg whites.

Spoon or pipe the meringue on to baking paper in the shape of a nest and bake at 100°C for at least 8 hours and preferably overnight. Or spoon or pipe the meringue on to baking paper in individual mounds — the mixture will make approximately 40 individual shells. The shells will take about 4 hours to bake.

Fill the large meringue nest with whipped cream and hulled strawberries. Leave the green stalks on some of the strawberries for decoration. Meringue is easier to slice if the cream and fruit are added 2 hours before serving. Keep in the fridge.

Try sandwiching the smaller meringue shells with whipped cream and Chocolate Ganache (p 19).

Your presentation will look more professional if you can pipe. Here is a quick lesson. Buy yourself a piping bag (the terylene type is easy to use), a large metal star-shaped nozzle, and a packet of instant mashed potato. Mix up the potato according to the instructions given on the packet. Place the nozzle in the piping bag. Fold the top of the bag down over your hand and spoon in about 8 large spoonfuls of mash. Twist the top of the bag so that the mash doesn't ooze out.

Now, using the hand that you write with to hold the back of the bag securely and firmly and the other hand to guide the metal nozzle, start piping rosettes along the kitchen counter.

The secret is to give firm pressure from the back of the bag and to press down. At my cookery school we were given the advice 'Start at 2 and finish at 10'. This makes sense if you imagine that you are piping over the face of a clock.

Mince Pies

Home-made mince pies melt in the mouth! Use a good quality shop-bought mincemeat that you have brightened up by adding a generous slurp of brandy, some grated apple, orange and lemon zest.

Even if making pastry fills you with dread, proceed! My recipe breaks most of the rules.

Pastry
300 g cake flour
generous pinch of salt
200 g cold butter, cut into pieces
1 jumbo egg yolk
iced water

The pastry can be made in a food processor but take care not to overmix. I make mine in a mixer using a K-beater. (You can make it by hand, but why rediscover the wheel?) Sift the flour into the bowl with the salt. Add the butter, cut into pieces. Mix until breadcrumb state, with a tea-towel over the top to prevent spillage.

Meanwhile mix the yolk with about 45 ml iced water. Add to the bowl, still mixing, adding a little more water as necessary until the mixture is a soft but firm dough.

Now, this is where my method is different:

I do not 'rest' the pastry in the fridge before rolling out. I find it makes the rolling out more difficult as it is not so easy to get the pastry thin, thin, thin. Roll out on a floured board with a floured rolling-pin. Keep the mince pie tins in the freezer before using so that they are icy cold, having first wiped them round with a piece of paper towel rubbed in softened butter. The chilled tins help to firm the pastry after rolling out.

Cut rings of pastry to fit the pie tins. Fill with mincemeat. Brush around the edges with egg yolk beaten with a drop of milk. Cut rings for the top and place over, sealing well. Brush with egg wash and make a small cross with a pointed knife in the top to allow the steam to escape. Bake in a preheated oven at 190°C until golden brown.

Sift castor sugar over the tops of the cooked mince pies. Only remove the pies from the tins after a few minutes as this will allow the pastry to firm up and reduce the risk of breakage. Cool on a rack.

Note :
If you haven't got pastry cutters, use an upturned wine glass. If you haven't got a rolling-pin, use a bottle.

To the uninitiated, a K-beater is a specific attachment for an electric mixing machine, just for making pastry. Use whatever attachment your mixer or processor recommends for pastry — but beware, go slowly. It's very easy to overmix with the magic fastness of the food processor.

Breakfast Muffins

The beauty of this mixture is that it can be kept in the refrigerator for up to 4 weeks; just make certain it is in a sealed, plastic container and when you come to use it, stir from the bottom up. Do not let the digestive bran put you off; it is easily available and very cheap and, of course, digestive bran is very good for you.

2 eggs
300 g brown sugar
approximately 80 ml oil
15 ml bicarbonate of soda (make certain the spoon is levelled off absolutely flat)
310 g flour
2,5 ml salt
500 ml digestive bran
500 ml milk
5 ml vanilla essence
125 g any kind of dried fruit (apricots, raisins, sultanas, etc.)

Cream the eggs and sugar together until light and fluffy. Add the oil and beat. Sift the bicarb, flour and salt together. Add the dry ingredients, milk and vanilla essence and mix very well. Add the fruit, cut into bite-sized pieces.

Spoon the mixture into oiled muffin tins and bake in a preheated oven at 180°C for 20 minutes.

These muffins are absolutely delicious eaten warm with butter and blackcurrant jam.

Mushrooms à la Greque

2 carrots, coarsely chopped
1 large onion, coarsely chopped
45 ml oil
125 ml white wine
salt and freshly ground black pepper
a bouquet garni (either a shop-bought one; or 2 sprigs parsley, 2 sprigs thyme and 2 bay leaves between 2 pieces of celery, all tied together with string)
1 big juicy clove of garlic, crushed
450 g mushrooms, sliced
225 g tomatoes, skinned, seeded and chopped (or if you use canned ones, drain very well after chopping)
30 ml parsley, chopped

The carrots and onions can be coarsely chopped together in the food processor, as they are going to be cooked together. Sauté the carrot and onion in the oil until they are soft. Add the white wine and season. Add the bouquet garni. Take care to tie it (whether fresh or dried) to the handle of the pan with a piece of string. This makes it easy to remove. Add the garlic and stir well. Add the mushrooms to the pan together with the tomatoes. Cook, uncovered, for 15-20 minutes.

Strain the contents of the pan. Return the liquid to the pan and boil vigorously until it is reduced by half. Remove the bouquet garni. Mix the solids back into the reduced liquid and chill.

Serve as a starter or as a salad, sprinkled with chopped parsley. 30 ml olive oil can be added when the mixture is cold.

Serves 6-8 as a starter.

Mussels in Curry Cream Sauce

30 g butter
1 onion, chopped
30 ml flour
7,5 ml curry powder
200 ml white wine
150 ml water
15 ml chopped garlic chives
salt and freshly ground black pepper
1 x 900 g can mussels in shells
10 ml lemon juice
75 ml cream
1 jumbo egg yolk

Melt the butter in a pan and sauté the onion until soft but not brown. Add the flour and curry powder and 'mellow' for 1-2 minutes. Then add the wine and water, a little at a time, beating well. Add the garlic chives and seasoning to taste. Finally, add the drained mussels and simmer gently for 5 minutes.

Beat the lemon juice, cream and egg yolk together. Add a little of the hot liquid from the pan and mix well. Remove the pan from the heat and add the egg yolk mixture. Stir well. Return to the heat, taking care not to let the mixture boil or it will curdle. When just heated through, serve immediately with hot, crunchy French bread.

Just makes a starter for 4.

Opposite: Mayonnaise
Overleaf: (left) Meringues and
(right) Omelette with four fillings
Page 50: Strawberry Phyllo Surprise
Prepared with choice ingredients from Woolworths food markets

Nectarine Dessert

When nectarines are out of season, use any fresh fruit. Why not try canned peach halves? I used to be snobby about canned fruit until Robert Carrier pointed out to the world that if they tasted canned peaches and were told they were a brand new brilliant discovery, they would appreciate them. It's only because we compare them with fresh peaches that we feel they are inferior — we should enjoy them in their own (taste) right.

The first time you make this dessert, take the time to fiddle and make the jam outline. It makes the dish look so professional. Chefs use heated, sieved strawberry or raspberry jam, but I use redcurrant jam as it has no pips. You will need a small piping bag and a small nozzle with a plain hole the size of a darning needle. Alternatively, go to a specialist supplier of cake-icing equipment and buy a packet of greaseproof paper piping bags. You can then throw the bag away after use. Clever people make their own greaseproof paper piping bags from double thickness greaseproof paper triangles made into a cone. If this sounds complicated just go out and buy some.

4 ripe nectarines
60 ml pure orange juice
60 ml white wine
50 g sugar (you can add a little more if you have a sweet tooth or if the fruit is sour)
45 ml Cointreau (we never said that being an Impatient Gourmet was cheap!)
2 kiwi fruit
redcurrant jam

Halve and skin the nectarines. The skins often come off easily without having to dip the fruit into boiling water. Place 2 halves on each serving plate, cut side downwards.

Meanwhile place the orange juice, wine and sugar in a small saucepan and bring to the boil. Simmer for 5 minutes. Remove from the heat and add the Cointreau.

Skin and slice the kiwi fruit and arrange decoratively around the nectarines. Using a piping bag and nozzle, trickle the jam in an outline around the fruit. If the jam won't come out of the nozzle easily, heat the jam for 20 seconds in the microwave. You don't want it boiling, otherwise when it is piped it will lose the outline effect. I find that most brands of jam work beautifully when cold as long as you stir them well before placing in the piping bag. It doesn't matter if your line wobbles — it looks even better. Trickle the orange juice sauce over the fruit and serve.

Serves 4.

Nutty Noodles

This noodle dish is simple and makes a delicious mate for chicken dishes.

Fresh breadcrumbs are easily made with the aid of a food processor. Just turn the machine on, using the metal blade, and add pieces of bread through the chute. Left-over breadcrumbs can be stored in a plastic bag in the freezer.

300 g ribbon noodles
60 ml butter
75 ml almond slivers
50 g fresh white breadcrumbs
freshly ground black pepper
parsley

Cook the noodles in boiling salted water to which you have added a spoonful of oil or a knob of butter — this prevents overboiling. Simmer the noodles until just cooked.

Meanwhile, melt the butter in a pan and add the almonds. Stir well and sauté for a minute or two. Add the breadcrumbs. Stir well and continue sautéing until golden and crisp.

Drain the noodles and mix in a serving dish with the almond and breadcrumb mixture, seasoning well with black pepper. Garnish with chopped parsley.

Serves 4.

O

Omelettes

(Illustrated on page 49)

The secret lies in having the right pan. The characteristic of an omelette pan is that it has a curved edge making it easier to turn the omelette out. An 18-21 cm pan is a good size, just right for a 4-egg omelette, enough for two people. A non-stick pan makes life easier.

Plain Omelette

4 eggs
salt
freshly ground black pepper
knob of butter (about 30 g)

Beat the eggs with the salt and pepper. Don't overbeat — just enough for the white and yolk to mix well. Put the pan on to a medium heat. Break the butter into two pieces and put into the pan. When frothing, pour in the egg mixture at once. Allow the mixture to begin to set and then stir round the edge of the omelette with the prongs of a fork, allowing the runny mixture on top to run on to the hot pan underneath. Keep going until you run out of the runny mixture.

Tilt the pan away from you and fold the omelette in half with the aid of a spatula. Have a warmed plate ready and tip the omelette straight on to it. The enclosed heat will have finished off the cooking of the inside of the omelette, but remember it is supposed to be slightly gooey. If you like it really set, cook for a minute longer before folding in half. Remember to eat the omelette immediately — it won't wait! If you have forgotten to warm the plates in the oven, just quickly pop them into hot water for instant heating.

Bacon and Potato Omelette

knob of butter (about 30 g)
2 medium-sized potatoes, diced
1 onion, finely sliced
3 rashers of bacon, cut into slices
salt and pepper
4-egg omelette recipe

Melt the butter in a pan, add the potatoes, onion and bacon. Season and cover the pan, cooking slowly until the potato and onion are done. Stir occasionally. Add to the 4-egg omelette before folding in half.

As a special topping, crumble some crispy, well-cooked bacon over the top of the omelette.

Cheese Omelette

This is my favourite!

Make a 4-egg omelette and scatter 30-45 ml grated cheese over the omelette when it is just on the point of setting. Fold over and the heat from the omelette makes the cheese all gooey. Sprinkle a little cheese over the top of the omelette. I use full-flavoured Cheddar cheese.

Chicken Liver Omelette

Super for Sunday evening supper.

3-4 chicken livers
knob of butter (about 30 g)
flour for dusting
dash of sherry
4-egg omelette recipe

Sauté the chicken livers in butter for 2 minutes. Dust with a little flour and add a dash of sherry. Simmer for 2-3 minutes. Add to a 4-egg omelette just before folding in half.

Mushroom Omelette

100 g mushrooms, sliced
knob of butter (about 30 g)
salt and freshly ground black pepper
4-egg omelette recipe

Sauté the mushrooms in the butter for 2-3 minutes. Season. Add to the 4-egg omelette just before folding in half.

Tomato Omelette

3 tomatoes, skinned, seeded and sliced
knob of butter (about 30 g)
salt and pepper
sprinkling of sugar
finely chopped mint
4-egg omelette recipe

Sauté the tomatoes in the butter in a pan for a minute or two. Don't overcook the tomatoes as this will make the mixture too wet. Season well, adding a sprinkling of sugar and finely chopped mint. Make the omelette the same way as the plain one and add the tomato mixture just before folding the omelette in half. Save a little for spooning on top of the omelette.

The easiest way to skin tomatoes is to sit them on paper towel in the microwave, cover with paper towel and give them 30 seconds on full power. Leave to stand for 5 minutes and then skin.

Orange and Lemon Water Ice

750 ml water
500 g granulated sugar
2 lemons (to yield 100 ml juice)
3-4 oranges (to yield 200 ml juice)
3 egg whites

Boil the water and sugar together for approximately 20 minutes to make a sugar syrup.

Meanwhile, remove some of the zest (outer yellow skin) of the lemon with a zester. It pulls the skin off in thin needles very easily. Zesters are available at all kitchen equipment shops and departments. Squeeze the lemons. Cut the oranges in half and with a pair of small, sharp pointed scissors, cut through the membranes of the oranges so that the juice and pulp can easily be removed with a grapefruit spoon. Remove any tough looking pieces of membrane, you just want the fruit juices and fruit pulp. Roughly chop the pulp. You will need 200 ml orange juice, excluding the fruit pulp.

Add the lemon zest to the pan with the syrup and cook for a minute or two to tenderise it and to bring out the full lemon flavour from the oils. Remove from the heat and add the orange juice and pulp. (At a pinch you can use 100% pure orange juice — the frozen variety — if you are in a rush.)

Freeze. Scrape the frozen water ice back into a roomy bowl. Whisk the egg whites until they start to form peaks (but are not dry) and fold into the frozen mixture. Refreeze.

This mixture looks good served in orange halves and having once done the scooping out of the shells, they can be washed after use and kept frozen, ready for action.

Serves 8.

An optional extra is to add a measure of Cointreau to the mixture. Do not be tempted to use bottled lemon juice.

Oxford Cream

A traditional dish from England — the very best, dark, rich marmalade must be used.

30 ml brandy
30 ml fresh lemon juice
350 g superb marmalade
600 ml cream

Stir the brandy and lemon juice into the marmalade. Whip the cream until stiff and fold into the marmalade mixture.

If you are really into home-made ice-cream, invest in a machine. It takes all the hassles out of ice-cream making and makes it extra smooth — in spite of the marmalade peel! If you have a machine, the mixture will freeze in about 30 minutes. Otherwise, cover and freeze for about 8 hours.

P

Paella

(Illustrated on front cover)

The perfect party dish! I cook this wonderfully easy dish over the braai in a huge old frying pan. The worst part is the pre-chopping.

Paella varies from region to region in Spain with many different ingredients being used. Pork can be added as well as crayfish — if you are feeling rich.

The spicy chorizo sausage is sometimes called chorico and is available at the deli section in the supermarket. If you have difficulty getting it, use a dry spicy garlicky sausage.

90 ml oil
1 chicken, cut into pieces
225 g chorizo sausage, sliced thickly
1 large onion, finely chopped
2 juicy cloves of garlic, crushed
1 x 400 g can tomatoes, drained and chopped
1 small can or 1 small jar of red pimentos (red peppers), drained and chopped
250 - 325 g uncooked rice
750 ml chicken stock
few threads of saffron
salt and freshly ground black pepper
cayenne pepper
60 ml parsley, chopped
8 large prawns, blanched
12 mussels in their shells, either cooked or canned
100 g frozen peas
dry white wine
wedges of lemon and black olives for garnishing

Heat the oil in a large frying pan over medium coals. Brown the chicken on all sides and sauté for approximately 5 minutes until partially cooked. You can do this ahead of time in the kitchen, if you prefer.

Add the chorizo sausage and sauté for a minute or two. Drain the chicken and chorizo, leaving the juices behind in the pan, and reserve. Add the onion to the pan and sauté until soft but not brown. Add the garlic, tomatoes and pimentos and sauté, taking care not to burn the garlic or it will impart a bitter flavour.

Next, add the rice, stirring well so that it turns golden and absorbs all the flavourful juices and fat. Mix the saffron with half the stock, stirring well. Add to the pan with salt, pepper, a sprinkling of cayenne and the parsley. Stir well. Remember, if you have used instant chicken stock, go easy on the salt.

Add the chicken, chorizo and prawns to the mixture, stirring lightly. Pour on the rest of the stock. Leave the paella to cook gently, uncovered, for approximately 15 minutes. Do not stir. Add the mussels and the peas, stirring gently. Cook for a further 5-10 minutes until the rice is fully cooked and all the liquid is absorbed. If any further liquid is required, and it will be, add some dry white wine.

Decorate with wedges of lemon and black olives.

Serves 8-10.

Pastry

Cheese pastry

I love this easy, rich cheesy pastry. I use it, cut into circles and crescents, for canapés for cocktail food — I particularly hate soggy toast bases! I've also used it as the base for savoury flans. Just try it ... it's delicious.

150 g cake flour
pinch of salt
150 g butter
150 g grated Cheddar cheese
5 ml dry mustard

This pastry can be made, easily, in a food processor or a mixer. Sift the flour and salt together. Add the butter, blend, and then add the cheese and mustard.

This is a very 'short' pastry. Knead until smooth. Wrap and chill for thirty minutes.

Roll out and use as required. Brush with egg yolk beaten with a little milk. Bake in a preheated oven at 190°C until golden brown.

I have a magic recipe for a quick Puff Pastry, but will save that for another book!

Shortcrust pastry

This is a basic pastry for pies, flans, etc. I'm giving you all 3 methods, including the hand method for all those people who aren't yet mechanised.

Processor method

Use the metal blade.

200 g cake flour
pinch of salt
100 g butter
1 jumbo egg yolk
icy-cold water

Place the flour and salt in the processor and turn on. Fluff the flour around for a minute and then stop and add the butter which should be cold and cut into pieces. Now be careful — don't overdo the timing. Turn the machine on and blend just until the mixture resembles breadcrumbs. If you are slap-happy, use the pulse switch, stopping every few seconds to check progress.

Mix the egg yolk with about 50 ml water. Turn the machine on and add the egg mixture through the chute, having more icy-cold water standing by. Add just enough water to make a soft dough. Don't overmix and don't make overwet, or you will have tough dough. Take it slowly and carefully. You want a soft manageable dough.

Now, every book tells you to chill the dough for at least 30 minutes. I find that it's easier to gently roll out the pastry straightaway and then to let it 'rest' in the fridge. Take your choice, though, as some experts feel that pastry will stretch if you roll it before 'resting'.

Cook in a preheated oven at 190°C.

Mixer method

I use a Kenwood Mixer with a K-beater and swear by it. When I had finished my training at the London Cordon Bleu School, I did a 3-year apprenticeship in a commercial kitchen with pastry being my main job for the first 6 months. Just try making 20 lbs shortcrust, 10 lbs puff, 5 lbs pâte sucrée and ... I used a Kenwood Major in that kitchen and we became very firm friends. I now use the smaller Kenwood Chef.

Take the same ingredients as for processor pastry.

Sift the flour and salt into the bowl. Cut the butter into pieces and place on the flour. Turn on the mixer at low speed with the K-beater. I put a tea-towel over the machine to prevent flour overspill but you can get a proper shield.

When the mixture resembles breadcrumbs (and don't rush it) add the egg yolk mixed with the water, adding more water if necessary. Remember, flour reacts differently each and every day so you can't be dead accurate with the amount of liquid required.

Hand method

Take the same ingredients as for the processor method.

Sift the flour and salt into a bowl. Make a well in the middle. Cut the butter into pieces and with cool hands (if they are hot, just soak them for a minute in iced water) work the butter into the flour mixture with the ends of the fingers. Continue until the mixture resembles breadcrumbs.

Knead in the egg yolk and water mixture, adding more water as necessary to get a soft manageable dough.

Devilled Pork

450 g belly of pork
100 ml tomato ketchup
30 ml Worcestershire sauce
30 ml vinegar
15 ml thin honey
salt and freshly ground black pepper
2,5 ml mustard
pinch of dried sage

Buy the belly of pork ready-sliced, or slice it evenly into 8 pieces. Remove the rind and any bones.

Combine the rest of the ingredients and stir well. Brush the slices of pork with this mixture and place them in a single layer in a shallow ovenproof dish. Pour over any remaining sauce. Cover with foil and bake in a preheated oven at 200°C for 40 minutes. Remove the meat from the oven and keep hot. Spoon or wipe off excess fat. Reduce the gravy by boiling rapidly and then pour it over the meat.

Serve with cabbage and baked potatoes in their jackets — delicious!

Serves 4.

Stuffed Pork Chops

Choose thick pork chops and cut through the fat side almost to the bone, so that a pocket is formed.

4 pork chops
45 ml butter
1 onion, finely chopped
75 ml fresh white breadcrumbs
5 ml dried sage
4 segments of orange chopped (if you are rushed for time, use canned mandarins)
grated rind of 1 orange
little orange juice
salt and freshly ground black pepper to taste

Melt the butter in a pan and sauté the onion until soft. Add the rest of the ingredients. Stuff the pork pockets with the mixture and secure with poultry pins.

Grill or roast in a preheated oven at 200°C for 10 minutes and then reduce to 180°C for approximately 25 minutes, or until done.

Serve with 150 ml fresh cream mixed with 20 ml lemon juice and 30 ml chopped chives.

Serves 4 — or, if you love meat, 2.

Pork Fillet Instant Dinner

This is my family's instant supper when I come home late. We have it on the table in just over half an hour — from start to finish.

1 pork fillet
flour
salt and freshly ground black pepper
60 g butter
6 spring onions, chopped
6 slices of lemon
100-125 ml dry white wine

Cut the fillet into 5 or 6 slices, depending on size. (Cut across the fillet, rather like cutting up a tree trunk.) Turn each slice with the cut side towards you, cover with plastic and bang it into an escalope with a meat banger, the end of a rolling-pin or the bottom of a milk bottle.

Dip the escalopes in flour seasoned with salt and freshly ground black pepper. Melt the butter in a frying pan until foamy and brown the escalopes on both sides. Turn the heat down and add the spring onions and the lemon slices. Grind in a little more black pepper and add the wine. Cook gently for approximately 10 minutes, turning the escalopes once. The wine should have evaporated to a sticky, tasty glaze.

Serve with a tossed green salad or tomatoes sliced with avocados, and Potato Mish-Mash (p 57).

Serves 4.

Potatoes

Château Potatoes — sort of

1 x 400 g can small potatoes
45 ml oil
45 ml butter
bacon, cut into slivers

Drain the potatoes well and dry with paper towel.

Heat the oil in a heavy pan and add the butter. Add the dried potatoes and fry over a high heat. When they are golden, add the slivers of bacon and cook until crispy.

Drain the potatoes and bacon well and serve garnished with sprigs of fresh mint.

They look and taste wonderful.

Serves 4.

Golden Crunchy Chips

The grandest restaurant chip never tastes as good as a home-cooked, straight-from-the-pan one.

Just follow the rules:

- Slice the potatoes into chips and soak in cold water for 30 minutes before frying.
- Dry the chips well — the easiest way to dry them is

in a lettuce whirler.

- Have a deep pan just over half-filled with fresh oil. (Never leave the kitchen when you have a pan of fat over heat.)
- If possible, use an electric deep-fat fryer as it seems to get to a higher, controlled temperature than a pan on top of the stove.
- Heat the oil until just below smoking temperature.
- When you add the uncooked chips, don't over fill the pan. Allow plenty of room for the chips to move.
- Do the chips in a number of batches.
- Fry them until cooked but not brown.
- Remove from the pan and drain.

All the above can be done earlier.

Shortly before serving time, heat the oil to smoking hot and brown the cooked chips. They brown fairly quickly. Drain on paper towel and sprinkle with salt.

Delicious Roasties

Peel and boil potatoes in salted water until cooked. Drain well and dry over the heat. Score the surface of the potatoes with a fork.

Place the potatoes in smoking fat in the top of the oven at 200 °C and turn well so that each potato is coated with fat. Cook until golden, turning once. Drain well on paper towel and sprinkle with salt.

If the smoking fat includes some true dripping, roast potatoes will be even more delicious.

Potato Mish-Mash

This is a method rather than a recipe.

Slice potatoes and onions very thinly in a food processor. Use approximately 2 potatoes for each medium-sized onion.

Heat some butter in a non-stick frypan and add the thoroughly mixed potato and onion mixture. Turn the mixture in the butter and add a generous knob on butter on the top. Put the lid on the frypan and reduce the heat to low.

After approximately 10 minutes turn the mixture, adding salt, pepper and a little dried tarragon. Add more butter if necessary. After about 20-25 minutes the mixture should be slightly brown on the bottom and have turned into a delicious potato and onion cake in the middle.

Tuna Stuffed Potatoes

This makes a wonderful supper dish when served with a salad. I make my own soured cream by mixing fresh lemon juice with fresh cream (see p 39).

4 large potatoes, scrubbed and pricked
1 x 200 g can tuna, flaked
30 g butter
150 ml soured cream
salt and freshly ground black pepper
125 g cheese, grated
125 g streaky bacon, chopped

Bake the potatoes at 180°C until tender. Or microwave — the time taken will vary, depending on the power of the microwave. If microwaving, remember to sit the potatoes on kitchen paper towel and also to cover them with paper towel. Halve the potatoes. Scoop out the flesh, keeping the shell intact. Mash the cooked potato and mix with the flaked tuna and its oil. Mix in the butter, soured cream and salt and pepper to taste. Spoon back into the potato shells. Top with grated cheese and chopped bacon. Place in an ovenproof dish and return to the oven at 200°C for 20-25 minutes, or pop under a hot grill. The cheese should be bubbly and the bacon crispy.

Makes a light meal for 4 — or a substantial meal for 2.

Spicy Fries

Delicious with crispy lamb chops.

500 g potatoes
oil
1 onion, chopped finely
15 ml mustard seeds
5 ml ground turmeric
10 ml curry powder
5 ml salt
pinch of ground chilli powder
45 ml fresh lemon juice
fresh coriander

Boil the potatoes in their skins until almost cooked. Skin and dice the potatoes. Heat a little oil in a pan and sauté the onion until golden. Add the mustard seed, turmeric, curry powder, salt and chilli powder. Stir into the onion and cook for a minute or two to 'mellow' the flavours.

Add the potatoes, stirring gently. Add the lemon juice and stir. Cook over a low heat. Add some chopped coriander leaves just before serving.

Serves 4.

Peri-Peri Prawns

Prawns make a quick gourmet feast. They are quickly deveined by cutting down the back of the prawn with a very sharp pair of scissors and removing the black vein with the tip of a knife.

1 kg prawns
175 ml oil
juice of 2 lemons
2 cloves of garlic, crushed
2 bay leaves
2,5 ml peri-peri (depending on your tastebuds)
2,5 ml celery salt
2,5 ml turmeric
2,5 ml curry powder
2 cloves

Mix all the ingredients together (except the prawns). Marinate the prawns in this mixture for about $1^1/_2$ hours, turning the prawns occasionally.

Cook the prawns in a pan in little hot oil and butter. Do not overcook. The time taken will depend on the size of the prawns. Heat the marinade and serve separately as a sauce.

Prawn Salpicon

Ideal for a starter, as a fishy treat on a buffet, or as a filling for savoury crêpes.

225 g prawns, without shells
60 g butter
1 onion, finely chopped
225 g tomatoes, skinned, seeded and chopped (canned are fine, but drain them well)
5 ml paprika (not some old paprika that has lost all its flavour)
15 ml tomato paste
pinch of sugar
salt and freshly ground black pepper

Make certain that the prawns have been deveined. Melt the butter in a pan. Add the onion and cook until soft but not brown. Add the tomatoes, paprika, tomato paste and sugar and stir well. (Don't leave out the sugar as it counterbalances the acidity of the tomato paste.)

If you are using fresh tomatoes, push the unused pulp through a sieve to get a little juice to add to the pan. But if you are using canned ones, don't worry as they will leak out quite a lot of juice. Add the prawns and the seasoning. Simmer gently for 3-4 minutes, depending on the size of the prawns.

This dish can be served hot or cold. Try serving it, chilled, in avocado halves or on a bed of red-leaf lettuce.

It is also excellent with cheesy rice. Just add grated cheese to hot, cooked, drained rice over a low heat until the cheese melts. Then mould into paper-lined ramekins. Unmould on to individual plates and spoon some prawn mixture around the base. Top with a spring onion.

Serves 4.

Easy Quiche

This is a method rather than a recipe. It's not a true quiche as too many bits have been added to it.

Make several at one go and keep the left-overs in the freezer.

Line a 20 cm flan ring with shortcrust pastry (p 55) and freeze for 30 minutes. For each 20 cm quiche chop up 4 rashers of bacon with a quarter of an onion. Cook together in a pan until the bacon is crispy and the onion soft. Add 1 clove of garlic, crushed. Allow to cool. Grate 100 g cheese.

Sprinkle the bacon, onion and garlic over the bottom of the pastry. Top with the cheese. Beat 2 jumbo eggs with 250 ml milk and cream mixed together. Season well. Pour over the cheese mixture and bake in a preheated oven at 190°C until the quiche is golden brown and seems fairly firm when shaken. It should take about 35-40 minutes. Spears of asparagus can be added, or a few spoonfuls of shelled cooked prawns.

The bacon, onion and garlic can be cooked very quickly in the microwave. Use a shallow dish and cover with paper towel. Try 2 minutes on full power — microwave until the bacon is crispy and the onion and garlic are cooked.

Ratatouille

Slightly different from most ratatouilles as I use tomato paste as a thickener.

Ratatouille is so versatile. Serve it chilled as a salad dish. Serve it as a starter, spooned into avocado halves. Serve it as a vegetarian dish, topped with grated cheese. Or as a hot vegetable companion to roast lamb. And, of course, it freezes well so it can be made when the ingredients are at their cheapest.

90 ml oil
2 onions, sliced
1 large green pepper, seeded and cubed
2 baby red peppers, seeded and cubed
1 large aubergine, sliced
5 courgettes (baby marrows), sliced
5 tomatoes, skinned, seeded and sliced (yes, you can use well-drained canned ones)
60 ml tomato paste
2,5 ml sugar
45 ml parsley, chopped
5 ml oregano
2,5 ml basil
2 large juicy cloves garlic, crushed
salt and freshly ground black pepper

Heat the oil in large pan and sauté the onion for 3 minutes. Add the rest of the vegetables and the tomato paste, stirring well. Cook for minute or two and then add the rest of the ingredients. Cook, uncovered, for approximately 25 minutes, stirring occasionally. Adjust seasoning.

If you are going to freeze the mixture, leave out the garlic as it can make the dish taste 'musty'. When it has thawed, reheat and add the garlic then.

Dirty Rice

The first 'dirty rice' I had in Louisiana, many years ago, used chicken giblet stock — and it was wonderful.

30 ml butter
375 ml brown rice
750 ml chicken stock
10 ml tomato paste (not purée)
Worcestershire sauce
Tabasco sauce
oregano
ground chilli
15 ml parsley, chopped
salt and pepper to taste

Melt the butter and stir in the rice. Cook for a minute or two, until golden. Keep stirring so that the rice doesn't catch. Gradually pour in the stock, stirring constantly.

Add the rest of the ingredients. The quantities depend on how hot you like your rice but start off with 2,5 ml

Worcestershire sauce, 2 drops Tabasco, 2,5 ml oregano and a sprinkling of chilli powder. Give the occasional stir. Simmer until the rice is just cooked.

Sufficient for 8.

Nutty Cheesy Rice

This rice is delicious with Prawn Salpicon (p 58) and also with roast lamb.

125 g rice, cooked
60 g butter
1 onion, finely sliced
salt and pepper
60 g cheese, grated
60 g almond slivers, lightly browned

Cook the rice by your usual method. Meanwhile, heat the butter and sauté the onion until soft but not brown. Add the rice. Season well and add the cheese and almonds. Stir well over heat until the cheese has melted.

Serves 4 as an accompaniment.

This rice can easily be moulded — it's because of its cheese content. Pack it into ramekins, timbales or ring moulds, keep it hot in the oven, and then unmould on to individual serving dishes.

On other occasions I have served it cold, moulded in a large ring mould. Then, having unmoulded it, I filled in the centre hole with Prawn Salpicon, decorated with some prawns in shells.

Wild Rice with Mushrooms and Celery

An ideal accompaniment to roast chicken, pork chops and Kassler chops.

1 box of brown and wild rice mixed (it comes 'cook in a bag')
60 g butter
125 g mushrooms, sliced
2 stalks celery, chopped
50 g slivers of almonds
salt and freshly ground black pepper

Cook the rice according to the instructions on the bag. Melt the butter in a pan and sauté the mushrooms and celery for 2-3 minutes. Brown the almonds in the oven or under the grill. Mix all the ingredients together and season to taste.

Serves 4.

Roquefort Cheese Pâté

500 g Roquefort cheese (or any blue-veined cheese)
500 ml white sauce
15 ml gelatine
45 ml brandy
150 ml thick cream
10 ml ready-made English mustard
cayenne pepper
100 g pecan nuts, chopped

Make the white sauce (see p 64 for my easy methods). Grate the cheese and mix with the white sauce while it is still hot.

Place the brandy in a small microwave dish and shake the gelatine over the top until it has been absorbed. Leave for 1 minute until it has 'caked'. Place in microwave for 35-45 seconds on full power. The mixture should be clear. (If you haven't got a microwave, use a small pan on top of the stove and melt the gelatine down over a very low heat.)

Add the dissolved gelatine to the cheese mixture, stirring well. Add the cream, mustard and cayenne to taste. Stir in the nuts and pour into a bowl or a mould.

Garnish with additional nuts and chopped parsley sprinkled either on top of the bowl or on top of the unmoulded pâté.

Roquefort Pasta

250 g pasta
30 ml butter
1 onion, finely chopped
125 g mushrooms, sliced
15 ml flour
125 ml Roquefort or any blue-veined cheese, crumbled
125 ml chicken stock
pinch of nutmeg
60 ml thick cream

Cook the pasta by your usual method taking care to add a little oil to the pan to avoid overspill.

Melt the butter in a pan and add the onion. Cook for a minute. Add the mushrooms. Cook for a further minute or two. Stir in the flour. Cook for another minute or two until the juices have been absorbed. Add the cheese, stock and nutmeg. Stir well to avoid lumps. Add the cream. Continue cooking until the sauce has thickened slightly. It is unlikely that salt and pepper will be needed but a little mustard could be added. Serve over the pasta.

Serves 4.

S

Sauces

Béarnaise Sauce

I'm giving you my microwave method. Of course, it can be made in the top of a double-boiler or, if you want to dice with death and risk curdling, make it over the direct heat but do have some iced water nearby. If it does curdle, you might be able to save it by adding 1-2 tablespoons of iced water off the heat and whisking like mad.

15 ml spring onions, chopped
2,5 ml dried tarragon, or 2 sprigs fresh tarragon, chopped
30 ml dry white wine
45 ml tarragon vinegar
few peppercorns
3 jumbo egg yolks
125 g butter
salt

Place the onions, tarragon, wine, vinegar and peppercorns in a microwave dish. Microwave, uncovered, until the liquid is reduced to half. (The time taken will depend on the dish and the microwave, but it could take as long as 5 minutes.)

Place the yolks in a food processor and blend thoroughly. Heat the butter in the microwave until very hot — absolutely bubbling. Add through the processor chute to the egg yolks while the machine is running. Strain the wine and vinegar mixture. Add through the chute too. Season with salt.

Just before using, place in a microwave dish and give the mixture 30-second blasts, whisking like mad between blasts, until it is hot — but be wary of overdoing it.

Serve immediately.

Makes enough for 6 people.

Bolognese Sauce

Top of the Stove and Microwave Methods.

What a versatile dish! Serve it on top of pasta; layer it with pasta, white sauce and cheese; stuff baked potatoes with it, or aubergines, or big tomatoes; layer it with parboiled sliced potatoes, or top it with creamed potato.

2 onions, sliced
15 ml oil
450 g minced beef
2 cloves garlic, crushed
100 g chicken livers, chopped
90 ml tomato paste
sprinkling of sugar
1 x 400 g can tomatoes, chopped and including the juice
1 bay leaf
5 ml oregano
5 ml basil
15 ml parsley, chopped
salt and freshly ground black pepper
100 ml instant beef stock

Top of the Stove Method

Sauté the onion in the oil in a large pan. Cook for 2 minutes, taking care that the onion doesn't burn. Add the minced beef a little at a time, pressing it down with a potato masher to iron out the lumps. Continue adding the beef and sauté until brown and separate. Add the garlic, stirring well. Add the chicken livers. Cook for a further few minutes. Add the tomato paste, stirring well. Add the sugar, tomatoes and juice, bay leaf, herbs and seasoning. Stir well.

Add the stock (half can be red wine, if it is available). Stir very well and allow to simmer for 30 minutes, uncovered. Remove the bay leaf and check the seasonings — chances are that they will require a little boost.

Microwave Method

Put the meat (without oil) in a large microwave dish and microwave on full power for 5 minutes. Stir a couple of times during cooking. Lift the meat out of the dish with a slotted spoon, leaving behind the juices and fat from the meat. Add the onions, garlic and chicken livers to the juices and stir. Microwave on full power for 2-3 minutes, stirring after each minute. Add the tomato paste and sugar. Stir and then add the rest of the ingredients as well as a peeled, cubed potato to help thicken the final sauce.

Return the meat to the mixture. And just in case you wonder why you took the meat out in the first place, cooking the chicken livers separately really does seem to make a difference to the flavour. Stir well, cover and microwave on full power for 9 minutes. The potato should be cooked but if it isn't, give the mixture a further minute or two. Refrigerate overnight.

Reheat by microwaving on full power for 3-4 minutes, stirring half-way through. Remove the bay leaf and adjust the seasoning. Hopefully the potato will have melted down and slightly thickened the sauce.

Makes enough for about 6 servings.

Bread Sauce

The secret with bread sauce is to allow the milk to 'infuse' with the flavour of the onion and cloves, and not to cook the breadcrumbs for too long — otherwise it will taste like a bread poultice.

1 large onion studded with cloves
1 bay leaf
250 ml milk
100 ml fresh white breadcrumbs
salt and pepper to taste
generous knob of butter
cream

Place the onion and bay leaf in the milk and bring to 'scalding' point (that's just before it boils when there are bubbles around the edge).

Remove from the heat, cover and leave for 1 hour. Remove the onion and bay leaf. Add the breadcrumbs and seasoning. Bring back to the boil and add the butter, whisking well. This can be reheated in the microwave.

Just before serving add a few spoonfuls of cream and stir. Microwave on full power for 2 minutes, stir and check temperature. A further minute should have it piping hot.

Makes enough to accompany 6-8 servings of turkey.

Champagne Sauce

(Illustrated on page 30)

This sauce, alone, could justify the purchase of a small basic microwave. It tastes divine. It enhances the richness of Christmas pud — cold or hot — and is outstanding with fresh strawberries or raspberries.

It can be made in the top of a double-boiler, or in a bowl over a pan of simmering water. But it takes forever. The microwave makes it quick and easy. But follow my instructions to the letter and do not leave the microwave during the cooking time to answer the telephone!

8 jumbo egg yolks (freeze the whites and use later for meringue)
100 g sugar (if you have a sweet tooth, you can increase it to 125 g)
1 dinky of sparkling dry wine (250 ml)

Beat the egg yolks until thick, thick, thick. Add the sugar, a little at a time, and continue beating. Turn the mixer down to low and add the wine, taking care to mix thoroughly from the bottom of the bowl.

Transfer into a large microwave bowl or jug. Microwave on full power for 2 minutes. Stand with your whisk at the ready. The moment the pinger goes, grab the bowl from the microwave and beat like crazy. Return the bowl to the microwave and give the mixture 30-second blasts, beating like mad in between each blast. This is vital as you don't want the mixture to curdle. Do not allow yourself to be distracted.

When the mixture has thickened, transfer the bowl to the counter and leave it there to cool. Every time you pass the bowl, give it a whisk. This ensures that the mixture doesn't separate. If you are serving it hot you don't have that problem. When the mixture is cold, cover with cling wrap and refrigerate.

This mixture should serve 6-8 people but don't be tempted to take tasters beforehand.

It sounds as if you need an astronaut's licence but it is so easy. I have had total non-cooks making it for me in my kitchen.

Chocolate Sauce

Be bothered! It's worth it.

110 g soft brown sugar
250 ml water
175 g dark chocolate, broken into pieces
grated rind and juice of 1 orange
60 g butter

Put the sugar and water into a small pan and bring to the boil, stirring well. Simmer for 10 minutes. Add the chocolate and orange rind and juice.

Over the gentlest heat (or in the microwave), heat sufficiently to melt the chocolate. Remove from the heat and whisk in the butter in flakes. This gives a wonderful shine.

This chocolate sauce can be made even more special with just 15 ml of Tia Maria, whisked in at the end.

Cumberland Sauce

Another sauce to brighten up Christmas left-overs. The perfect mate for ham, all year round.

1 jar redcurrant jelly
grated rind and juice of 1 orange and 1 lemon
150 ml red wine
15-25 ml cornflour or arrowroot (arrowroot is available at some supermarkets)

Mix the jelly, rind, juice and red wine together and bring to the boil. Mix the cornflour or arrowroot with a little water. Add to the pan, stirring briskly. Cook for a minute or two. As a luxury touch — and it certainly is with the present price of liqueurs — add 30 ml Grand Marnier.

The variation in the quantity of cornflour or arrowroot is to take into account the amount of juice the orange and lemon yield.

Cranberry Orange Relish

Quickie sauces and relishes 'tiddle up' boring left-overs. This one is great with cold ham and cold turkey.

60 ml water
125 ml orange juice
225 g castor sugar
*2 cans cranberries (unsweetened)**
grated rind of 2 oranges

(*If you have to use sweetened canned cranberries, leave out the sugar and taste for sweetness at the end. If very sweet, add a little fresh lemon juice.)

Heat the water, orange juice and castor sugar together, stirring continuously until the sugar is dissolved. Add the cranberries and juice, followed by the orange rind. Simmer until heated through. Remove from the heat and allow to cool.

Chill for at least 2 hours before serving.

White Sauce

I'm an Impatient Cook too — haven't you guessed by now? Funnily enough, I haven't the patience to make a white sauce by the microwave method, even though I'm the microwave's greatest fan when it comes to egg-based sauces. But with a White Sauce (and, if you have the time, the true Béchamel) it's just so easy on the top of the stove that I really can't be bothered with all the 'ins and outs' of the microwave method. (I *can* be bothered with a champagne sauce because it takes so long on top of the stove — if you don't want it to curdle — that I go to sleep!)

Back to the White Sauce.

By the way, it becomes a Béchamel, which is so superior, if you bother to 'infuse' the milk. I know it sounds painful, but all it means is that you plonk some goodies into the milk before bringing it all to 'scalding' point. And who knows what that means? You do of course because hereby hangs a lesson ...

(No, I don't always bother... especially not when I come through the door, late in the evening, to find many a hungry eye accusing me.)

If there is time, take
125 ml milk
slice of onion
slice of carrot
6 peppercorns
bay leaf
1 blade of mace (this is the outer husk of the nutmeg, and I promise it makes a difference; yes, you can get it at specialist shops — otherwise leave it out)

Put all the ingredients in a pan, place over heat and bring to 'scalding point'. That means when bubbles appear around the edge of the milk, just prior to its boiling. Immediately remove from the heat, and cover. Leave for at least 30 minutes. One hour is better. Then strain.

Now take 30 ml (30 g) butter and melt it in a pan. Throw in a little extra knob of butter. It makes sauce-making so much easier. Add 30 ml flour. Cook over heat, 'mellowing' the flour. Stir until it has absorbed all the butter and has slightly changed colour.

This is the secret of sauce-making. Add the milk, a little at a time, first stirring with a spoon and then (and once again this is vital) beating with a whisk. When all the milk has been added, continue cooking until the sauce has thickened, beating constantly with the whisk.

I promise, you will not have lumps. It only takes minutes and if you are short of time don't even think of infusing the milk.

It's even easier in the microwave.

Melt the butter in a largish dish on full power for 40 seconds. Add the flour and stir well. Microwave on full power for 45 seconds. Add the milk, beating well. Microwave on full power for 1 minute. Beat well. Repeat. Repeat a third time and it's perfect.

Savoury Butters

Savoury butters have a whole host of delicious uses but are particularly good as toppings for steaks and fillings for savoury bread.

Anchovy Butter

125 g butter
6 anchovy fillets
freshly ground black pepper
anchovy sauce to taste

Blend all the ingredients together in a food processor. If you haven't got a food processor, soften the butter on a plate with the blade of a knife. Crush or pound the anchovies, adding these to the butter with the freshly ground black pepper and anchovy sauce.

Serve with lamb chops, fish or steak.

Delicious Topping For Grilled Steak

Mix 60 ml butter with 15 ml French mustard and spread this mixture over the steaks. Grill the normal way but for the last period of cooking time sprinkle brown sugar over the meat and cook until glazed. When serving, be certain to pour the pan juices over the meat.

Makes enough for 4 steaks.

Garlic Butter

3 cloves of garlic
125 g butter
15 ml lemon juice
30 ml chopped parsley

Crush the garlic and add to the butter, lemon juice and parsley in the food processor or mix together with the blade of a knife. Place the mixture on greaseproof paper and roll up like a Swiss roll. Twist the ends of the paper to secure. Chill until hard. Remove the paper and cut into slices. Serve with steaks.

Parsley Butter

125 g butter
75 ml chopped parsley
generous squeeze of lemon juice

Blend all the ingredients together in a food processor or mix together with the blade of a knife. Place the mixture on greaseproof paper and roll up like a Swiss roll. Twist the ends of the paper to secure. Chill until hard. Remove the paper and cut into slices. Serve with any meat.

Smoke Cookery

Even an Impatient Cook can usually stand the trauma of lighting a braai.

The origins of smoke cookery are far, distant and misty. We do know that the American Indians were magnificent smokers: they gutted their catch of fish, rubbed it with salt, impaled it on long sticks and cooked it over dense, hot smoke. The fish was tilted, easel-fashion, against a stake pounded into the ground near the fire and slowly, as the hours passed, it cooked beautifully and became impregnated with the dark taste of fine wood smoke. This method is still used in Argentina.

Smoke cookery utilises a hot fire and hot smoke and is intended to cook the meat or fish as well as flavour it. Meats treated this way do not need to be marinated although that would certainly make for interesting eating. Start with a wood or charcoal fire, then smother it with damp wood chips to produce a dense smoke. The best flavour is imparted by sweet woods — avoid resinous woods such as pine. Commercially packaged chips are available. You may also sprinkle fresh or dried herbs over the burning chips to produce additional flavours. Here is a basic marinade for preparing meat for smoking.

125 ml soy sauce
125 ml water
125 ml honey
250 ml sherry
5 ml cinnamon
5 ml pepper
2,5 ml ground cloves
125 ml strong black tea
2 juicy, crushed cloves of garlic

Mix all the ingredients together. Small food items will only need marinating for a few hours. Larger ones will taste better if soaked overnight. Even ingredients such as chicken livers, hamburgers, sausages and spare ribs will be delicious if marinated in this mixture and then smoked.

Smoked Mussel and Haddock Pâté

2 x 125 g cans smoked mussels in cottonseed oil
250 ml cream of smoked haddock soup (if not easily available, substitute 250 ml smooth cottage cheese or 1 x 425 g can cream of mushroom soup)
1/2 bunch spring onions, chopped
125 ml mayonnaise
125 ml cream, lightly whipped
Tabasco sauce
cayenne pepper
salt and freshly ground black pepper
20 ml gelatine
45 ml lemon juice

Place the smoked mussels (including their oil), soup and spring onions in a food processor. Blend. Add the mayonnaise, cream, a dash of Tabasco and seasonings and blend well. Meanwhile place the lemon juice in a small dish and shake the gelatine over the top until it has been absorbed. Leave to 'cake'. Place in the microwave for 30-40 seconds on medium power until transparent but do not let it boil. Add to the mussel mixture and blend well. Pour into ramekins. When set, unmould and garnish with curled spring onion.

If you want to unmould — and remember you don't have to — it makes life easier if you first line the base of the ramekin with a piece of oiled greaseproof paper.

Serves 8.

Opposite: Syllabub
Overleaf: Vegetable Curry
Prepared with choice ingredients from Woolworths food markets

Smoked Salmon Mousse

Luxurious but divine. This recipe can also be used for smoked trout mousse. The microwave method is the easiest.

175 g Philadelphia cream cheese
finely grated rind of 1 lemon
3 egg yolks
325 ml cream
salt and freshly ground black pepper
cayenne pepper
1 clove garlic, crushed
175 g smoked salmon (trimmings can be used)
60 ml finely chopped parsley
175 g fresh breadcrumbs

Put the cheese, lemon rind, egg yolks and cream in the top of a double-boiler. Remember when you use a double-boiler that the water in the lower pan must not touch the base of the upper pan. The idea is that the food is gently cooked in steam.

Stir the mixture continuously until smooth and slightly thickened. Remove from the heat. Season with salt, pepper, cayenne pepper and crushed garlic.

Chop the smoked salmon very finely and add to the mixture with the chopped parsley and breadcrumbs.

Spoon into individual soufflé dishes, ramekins or a lined bread tin. Set in the refrigerator.

Serve with a garnish of fresh herbs and a slice of lemon.

Microwave Method

Microwave the cheese mixture on full power for 1 minute. Beat well and microwave for further 30-second blasts, mixing well in between, until the mixture starts thickening. Continue as before.

Serves 6-8.

Soups

Curried Apple Soup

Chilled soups need a lot of seasoning so that they don't taste insipid. Remember to taste, taste, and taste again.

30 ml butter
1 onion, coarsely chopped
15 ml curry powder
500 ml chicken stock
15 ml cornflour
125 ml cream
2 egg yolks
3 large apples, peeled, cored and sliced
salt and freshly ground black pepper
juice of 1/2 lemon
watercress or parsley for garnish

Melt the butter, add the onion and cook until soft but not brown. Add the curry powder and cook for a minute or two to 'mellow'. Stir in the stock and bring to the boil. Add the cornflour mixed with a little water.

Bring back to the boil and simmer for a few minutes. Heat the cream. Add the egg yolks to the hot cream and stir gradually into the hot soup. Do not overheat or the mixture will curdle.

Remove from the heat and transfer to the food processor with 2 of the prepared apples and blend until smooth. Season to taste with salt and pepper. Add the lemon juice and chill.

Garnish with watercress or parsley and chopped apple.

Serves 4.

Curried Turkey Soup

This is a method rather than a recipe and is one of my family's favourites.

Take the carcass of the turkey and break or cut it into pieces. Hopefully there will still be some flesh left on it. Place it in a large stockpot.

Meanwhile gently sauté 30 ml finely chopped onion, 2 cloves of crushed garlic, 2,5 ml ground turmeric, some slivers of fresh ginger and a generous pinch of ground chillies in 50 g butter. These are the quantities per litre of water used. Add the water and bring to the boil. Pour on to the turkey carcass and simmer very slowly for 2 hours. Remove the bones and season with salt and lemon juice.

French Onion Soup

250 g onions
60 g butter
a little sugar
1,5 litres beef stock
salt and freshly ground black pepper
125 ml brandy (optional)
toasted French bread
grated cheese

Slice the onions finely. Heat the butter in a large frying pan with a sprinkling of sugar. Add the sliced onions and cook until golden brown. If you try to do this in a casserole, steam goes back into the mixture and the onions won't brown. Pour in some of the stock, stirring continuously.

Transfer to a casserole or stockpot. Add the rest of the stock and simmer gently for an hour. Do not add any salt at this stage if you have used stock cubes, as they tend to be salty.

Check the seasoning and add some freshly ground black pepper. Just before serving, add the brandy.

Place a slice of toasted French bread, topped with grated cheese, in each serving bowl, and pour the soup over it. Bake in a preheated oven at 230°C until the cheese is bubbling and golden brown.

Allow 250-300 ml of soup per person.

If you have very large soup bowls, it pays to measure them. Nothing looks worse than a little soup lurking at the bottom of a huge bowl, but do remember that you are serving it with French bread.

Pumpkin and Tomato Soup

This soup can be served hot or chilled. Allow 250 ml per head.

500 g pumpkin, skinned, seeded and chopped
3 large onions, chopped coarsely
1 x 400 g can tomatoes
750 ml instant chicken stock
1 large bay leaf
250 ml cream
salt and freshly ground black pepper
for garnish:
125 ml lightly whipped cream
chopped chives, chopped garlic chives or chopped ends of spring onions

Put the pumpkin, onions, tomatoes and their juice, stock and bay leaf into a pan. Bring to the boil and simmer for 30 minutes. The vegetables should now be soft. Add the cream and plenty of pepper and sufficient salt (remembering that instant stock is inclined to be salty) to give a good flavour. Liquidise in a food processor or liquidiser/blender.

If serving hot, add a dollop of whipped cream topped with a sprinkling of chopped chives, garlic chives or spring onion tips.

If serving chilled, keep the serving bowls in the fridge, along with the soup. Just before serving, garnish as for the hot soup.

Serves 4-6.

Salmon Soup

1 onion, finely chopped
30 ml butter
60 ml flour
500 ml chicken stock
375 ml milk
1 x 425 g can condensed tomato soup
1 large can salmon (or 2 small cans)
Worcestershire sauce
2,5 ml sugar

salt, cayenne and black pepper
125 ml cream, beaten until just holding its shape
chopped chives or garlic chives

Gently sauté the onion in butter until transparent but not browned. Add the flour and cook for a few minutes, stirring well. Gradually add the chicken stock, stirring well to avoid lumps, and then add the milk, tomato soup and the salmon (from which the black skin and bones have been removed). Simmer for approximately 5 minutes.

Add a generous dash of Worcestershire sauce and the sugar. Season to taste with salt, cayenne and black pepper. Blend in a blender / liquidiser or food processor.

Chill well in the refrigerator, and just before serving add the lightly beaten cream and chopped chives or garlic chives.

Serves 6.

Barbequed Spare Ribs

1,5 kg spare ribs
1 large onion, finely chopped
30 ml oil
1 clove garlic, crushed
100 ml tomato paste
45 ml lemon juice
2,5 ml salt
2,5 ml pepper
60 ml brown sugar
125 ml chicken stock
60 ml Worcestershire sauce
10 ml dry mustard

Cook the spare ribs by boiling gently in water for 30 minutes. Drain.

Sauté the onion in the oil for 2-3 minutes. Add the remaining ingredients. Simmer for 3 minutes. Cool and marinate the spare ribs in this sauce overnight.

Remove the spare ribs from the marinade and braai over hot coals. Turn them over two or three times while cooking and baste frequently with the marinade.

Heat the remaining marinade and pour it over the cooked spare ribs. Garnish with onion curls.

How many people will this dish feed? Depends on how mad you are about spare ribs but it should be enough for 4 hearty trenchermen.

Strawberry Phyllo Surprise

(Illustrated on page 50)

The surprise is that this is almost an instant dessert but looks so professional. You need phyllo or fillo pastry, which is available at many supermarkets as well as specialist Greek delis.

Keep the phyllo in the freezer until you need it. It thaws out in about 1½ hours — but keep it covered with a damp cloth to prevent drying out.

Carefully unroll the layers of pastry. Decide whether you are going to make small individual desserts, a large round one or an oblong. Then cut out layers of the pastry accordingly. For a large ring, use a saucepan lid as a guide. For a small round, use a large wine glass.

Heat oil (for deep fat frying) to just below smoking point in a heavy-based pan. Fry the pastry shapes on both sides until golden and drain on paper towel. This can be done up to an hour before you need them provided you keep them somewhere free from steam. (Try popping them on the guest room dressing-table.)

Just before serving, layer with whipped cream and strawberries. Sift icing sugar over the top layer. Three layers is the minimum and five layers the maximum. If you have a very sweet tooth, sweeten the strawberries with sifted icing sugar.

One commercial roll of phyllo pastry will make about 10 three-layer individual desserts.

Syllabub

(Illustrated on page 67)

rind and juice of 1 large lemon (it should yield about 60 ml)
20 ml brandy
30 ml medium sherry
75 g icing sugar
375 ml cream

Do make certain to get the yellow part of the lemon skin as it contains very flavourful oils. Leave the white pith behind as it gives a bitter taste. If you haven't got a zester, use a swivel potato peeler.

Soak the lemon rind with the juice, brandy and sherry for at least 2 hours. It doesn't really matter how long it stands. Strain the liquid into a mixing bowl and beat in the sugar. Stir until dissolved. Add the cream, a little at a time, beating well. Continue beating until the mixture thickens. Either spoon or pipe into wine glasses. Chill.

Serve with a boudoir biscuit and a few slivers of lemon rind.

Serves 6.

Taramasalata

This recipe will horrify most Greeks as I use cream in it. But it tastes delicious!

12 slices white bread, crusted
125 ml cream
1 jar or carton (about 150 g size) tarama (salted cod's roe)
½ onion, chopped coarsely and blanched in boiling water for 2 minutes
2-3 cloves garlic, crushed
juice of 1 lemon
125 ml oil
lemon slices and olives for garnish

Soak the bread in the cream. Place in a food processor together with the tarama, onion, garlic and lemon juice. Blend, adding the oil through the chute. If the mixture is a little thin, add more bread. Blend until smooth.

Garnish with lemon slices and olives and serve with Toast Melba (see below) as a starter or as a dip for cocktail parties.

This dish freezes well.

At the risk of upsetting the canners, I must admit I have never found a really good canned cod's roe. They all seem very bland.

Toad-in-the-Hole

Toad-in-the-hole usually consists of sausages cooked in a tasty, golden batter, but originally pieces of meat were used instead of the sausages, and you can easily substitute partially cooked lamb chops (about one-third cooked).

The batter is obviously an important part of the dish, and I am giving a prize-winning recipe from a Yorkshire Pudding Competition held in England about 5 years ago. To everyone's surprise, a man won the competition — and a Chinese gentleman to boot! His name was Tin Sung Chan and he came from Hong Kong. The panel of judges found his method of making the Yorkshire pudding unorthodox, but considered the end-product absolutely right for the perfect Yorkshire pudding. In the original ingredients for the Yorkshire pudding batter, Tin Sung Chan included half a teaspoon of Tai Luk sauce, and everyone went mad trying to obtain it. Eventually, a Chinese shopkeeper explained the joke: Tai Luk translated means Mainland China!

Batter:
300 ml milk
4 eggs
2,5 ml salt
dash of pepper
250 g cake flour
pork sausages (allow 2 robust pork sausages per person for the average appetite)

Make the batter by beating the milk, eggs, salt and pepper together in a food processor or blender/liquidiser until lots of bubbles show on the surface. Leave to stand for 15 minutes. Then sift the flour and whisk it into the mixture.

Meanwhile, fry or grill the pork sausages until partly cooked. Preheat the oven to 220°C and also preheat an oven dish with a little oil in it. Remove the oven dish from the heat, and pour in a thin layer of batter. Cook in the oven for approximately 5 minutes until the batter is set. Place the sausages on top and pour over the rest of the batter. Bake for 30-35 minutes until golden and puffed.

Toast Melba

It browns very quickly, so don't look away for a second. Toast Melba stores beautifully in airtight containers.

Use shop-sliced white bread and toast on both sides. Remove three crusts and, with a sharp knife, slice through the inside of the bread (between the two toasted sides, like opening the leaves of a book), making two slices, both brown on one side and white on the other. Then cut off the last crust which has acted as an anchor.

Place on a baking sheet, untoasted side uppermost, and place in a preheated oven at 100°C until curled. Remove from the oven and brown the white side of the bread under the grill.

Brown bread can also be used.

Braai Tomato Special

This tomato special turns even braaied boerewors into gourmet fare.

1 onion, sliced
1 x 400 g can tomatoes, chopped
2 cloves garlic, crushed
grated rind and juice of 1 orange
sprinkling of sugar
salt and freshly ground black pepper
1 bay leaf
10 ml Worcestershire sauce
2 drops Tabasco sauce

Mix all the ingredients together and simmer until the onion is cooked and the mixture is thick. Wonderful with boerewors and 'pap'.

Stuffed Tomatoes

This is a pleasant starter, a simple Sunday supper dish, or ideal for serving to a vegetarian.

1 tomato per person
stuffed with:
20 ml fresh brown breadcrumbs (made by pushing pieces of bread through the chute of the processor while the motor is running)
crushed garlic (1 clove to 6 tomatoes)
2,5 ml chopped parsley
7,5 ml Parmesan cheese
sprinkling of dried tarragon
sprinkling of oil
freshly ground black pepper
dash of Worcestershire sauce

Cut the top off each tomato — the opposite end to where it has been pulled off its stalk. With some kitchen scissors snip around the inner core, scooping out quickly and easily with a grapefruit spoon. If you haven't got one, use a teaspoon. Reject any coarse bits of core and put the rest of the tomato pulp in a bowl.

Combine with the rest of the ingredients. Stuff back into the tomato. Put the 'lid' firmly back on the tomato and pack the tomatoes tightly into a shallow casserole. Cover with foil or a lid and bake in a preheated oven at 180°C for approximately 30 minutes until the tomatoes are cooked through. The time obviously depends on the size of the tomatoes.

This dish can also be done in the microwave. Try 5 - 7 minutes on full power for 6 medium-sized tomatoes.

Sunflower Tomatoes

8 button mushrooms
sweet pepper dressing (see p 31)
8 large firm tomatoes
1 curly endive or red lettuce
salt and pepper

Remove the stalks from the mushrooms. Marinade the mushroom caps in the sweet-pepper dressing overnight. To arrange the salad, cut each tomato into 6 segments, taking care not to slice right through to the base. Open carefully like a flower. Place each tomato on a bed of endive or red lettuce and season with salt and pepper. Sit a mushroom in each tomato, and coat with sweet-pepper dressing.

As an individual salad dish serves 6-8.

Torrijas

You are not to tell anyone what they are really eating. They usually think it's cinnamon doughnuts. Don't try to eat them cold though — they are revolting.

450 g icing sugar, sifted with 30 ml fresh, powdered cinnamon
3 jumbo eggs
250 ml sweet sherry
very new bread, approximately 2 cm thick, cut into 6 cm circles — obviously crustless!

Place the icing sugar and cinnamon in a bowl. In a second bowl beat the eggs thoroughly to mix the yolks and the whites. Have the sherry in a third bowl.

Pull the bread through the sherry first, then through the egg mixture. Fry immediately in fresh, hot oil. Put them straight into the icing sugar mixture, coating them very well.

Serve immediately — no waiting!

The number of servings will depend on how many slices of bread you cut up — or how hungry you are.

Trifle with a difference

1 large jam Swiss roll
75 ml sweet or medium sherry
6 kiwi fruit, peeled and sliced
100 g boudoir biscuits, broken
50 g almond nibs
3 egg whites
125 g castor sugar
150 ml semi-sweet white wine
30 ml brandy
15 ml lemon juice
250 ml cream
additional cream, nuts and kiwi fruit to decorate

Slice the Swiss roll and arrange in a large glass bowl. Moisten with the sherry. Place the kiwi fruit over the Swiss roll and top with the broken boudoir biscuits. Sprinkle with almonds. Whisk the egg whites until stiff and then gradually add the sugar, whisking until firm and glossy. Add the wine, brandy and lemon juice, gently folding them into the sugar mixture.

Whip the cream until softly stiff and fold into the sugar mixture. It sounds complicated but it really is easy. Pour over the Swiss roll and fruit mixture. Cover and refrigerate for 2 hours. Just before serving decorate with cream, nuts and fruit.

6 very generous servings.

Trout Père Louis

The slurp of brandy, Grand Marnier and cream topped with toasted almonds, makes Trout Père Louis a quickie winner.

4 trout
60 ml butter
90 ml cream
30 ml Grand Marnier
30 ml brandy
salt and freshly ground black pepper
30-60 ml toasted flaked almonds

Melt the butter in a frying pan and gently fry the trout for about four minutes on each side (time obviously depends on the size of the trout). The eyes go opaque when the trout are cooked. Heat the cream in a separate saucepan without letting it come to the boil. Stir in the Grand Marnier and brandy and season with salt and pepper. Heat through until just below boiling.

Place the trout on a warm serving dish and coat with the sauce. Sprinkle with the browned flaked almonds and serve immediately.

Serves 4.

Roasting the Christmas Turkey

If you are using a frozen bird, remember that it doesn't thaw out overnight. Let it thaw in the fridge and allow 2 days.

Quick Method

Turn the oven on to maximum — 230°C. Rub the turkey with butter and seasoning — even if it is a self-basting bird (incidentally, they are deliciously moist). Place the turkey in the oven in a roasting pan and the moment it is brown remove it from the oven and wrap it, 'mummy-like', in rashers of bacon. Cover with foil, shiny side inwards, and return to the oven. The turkey should be covered loosely but completely sealed with the foil.

Here is a cooking chart — remember the initial cooking time is counted in the total cooking time.

3½ - 4½ kg — 2½ - 2¾ hours
4½ - 5½ kg — 2¾ hours - 2 hours, 50 minutes
5½ - 6½ kg — 2 hours, 50 minutes - 3 hours
6½ - 7½ kg — 3 - 3¼ hours
7½ - 8½ kg — 3¼ - 3½ hours

To check if the turkey is done, pierce the thickest part of the thigh with a skewer or poultry pin. If the juices run clear, it is done. If they run pink, it needs more time. Allow the turkey to stand for 30 minutes before carving. It really does make the carving easier.

Slow Method

Rub the turkey with butter, salt and freshly ground black pepper. Cover loosely with foil. Cook in a preheated oven at 170°C.

Cooking chart:

$3^1/_2$ - $4^1/_2$ kg	—	$3^1/_2$ - $3^3/_4$ hours
$4^1/_2$ - $5^1/_2$ kg	—	$3^3/_4$ - 4 hours
$5^1/_2$ - $6^1/_2$ kg	—	4 - $4^1/_4$ hours
$6^1/_2$ - $7^1/_2$ kg	—	$4^1/_4$ - $4^1/_2$ hours
$7^1/_2$ - $8^1/_2$ kg	—	$4^1/_2$ hours - 4 hours, 50 minutes

Remove the foil approximately 45 minutes before the end of the cooking time. Baste well and raise the oven temperature to 200°C in order to brown the bird.

With either method, turn the bird over half-way through. Save the juices for gravy.

Turkey Stuffings

Remember:

Stuffings should always be made in advance so that they have a chance to cool. If hot stuffings are put into turkey cavities they can turn the bird sour.

The easy way to stuff the bird is to place the stuffing in a piping bag (no nozzle please) and just squeeze the mixture into the bird's cavity. No mess — it's very easy.

Celery, Apricot and Pecan Stuffing

1 large onion, finely chopped
60 g butter
2 sticks celery, chopped
60 g dried apricots, soaked overnight
100 g pecans, chopped
15 ml parsley, chopped
350 ml fresh breadcrumbs
salt and pepper to taste
1 jumbo egg
sherry

Sauté the onion in the butter until soft but not brown. Remember, if onion goes into the stuffing uncooked it never seems to soften fully inside the bird. Add the celery, drained apricots, nuts, parsley, breadcrumbs and seasonings. Mix well. Beat the egg and add to the mixture with enough sherry to make a moist stuffing.

Microwave Method

Place the onion and the butter in a microwave dish. Cover with cling wrap and microwave on full power for 2 minutes. Add the celery, drained apricots, nuts, parsley, breadcrumbs and seasonings. Mix well. Beat the egg and add to the mixture with enough sherry to make a moist stuffing.

The above quantities will make enough stuffing for one end of a 4 kg turkey.

Chestnut Stuffing

50 g bacon, chopped
50 g butter
100 g fresh breadcrumbs
15 ml parsley, chopped
grated zest and juice of 1 lemon
500 g chestnut purée (canned is fine but make sure it is unsweetened)
salt and pepper to taste
1 jumbo egg

Fry the bacon until crisp. Crumble. Mix with the butter, breadcrumbs, parsley, lemon juice and zest and chestnut purée. Season and add the beaten egg. If the mixture seems dry, add a little sherry.

The above quantities will make enough stuffing for one end of a 4 kg turkey.

Unbelievably Easy Crème Brûlée

This is my friend Dorianne Berry's recipe so it really should go under D or C — but I needed a U.

1 x 410 g can evaporated milk, well chilled
2 packets instant vanilla pudding
250 ml cream
castor sugar

Beat the first three ingredients together until thickening. Pour into a shallow, ovenproof dish. Chill. Top with a thick layer of castor sugar — the amount you need will depend on the size of the dish. Place under a red hot grill until the sugar caramelises. Chill in the fridge for 4 hours.

Serves 6.

Vegetable Casserole

1 very large potato, peeled
2 sticks celery
2 carrots
2 tomatoes
2 patty pans
3 green beans
90 ml grated cheese
black pepper
1 x 425 g can condensed mushroom soup
100 ml cream

Slice the vegetables thinly. It helps if you have a food processor. Layer in a shallow casserole. Sprinkle the cheese, mixed with some freshly ground black pepper, on top of the vegetables. Mix the soup with the cream and pour over the vegetables. Bake in a preheated oven at 180°C for 35-40 minutes. It's important to slice the vegetables thinly.

If you are in a tearing rush, cover with cling wrap and microwave on full power for 15 minutes and then finish in the oven at 200°C until golden and bubbly.

Serves 2 as a supper dish and 4-6 as an accompanying vegetable dish.

Vegetable Curry

(Illustrated on page 68)

My husband lived in India for 2 years, so he makes the curries in our house. It is his only culinary skill — and it is a superb one.

Any selection of fresh vegetables, such as
5 courgettes (baby marrows)
1 aubergine (brinjal)
5 baby sweetcorn
12 mangetout (snow peas)
10 green beans
5 patty pans
peas
2 potatoes
3 tomatoes
1 green pepper
1 red pepper
It's really a matter of what's available.

45 ml oil
1 large onion, chopped
2 cloves garlic, crushed
15 ml ground coriander
10 ml turmeric
2,5 ml ground chilli powder
2,5 ml ground cumin
2,5 ml ground ginger
2,5 ml ground mustard seed (but I sometimes use it whole)
pinch of ground fenugreek (optional)
1 x 400 g can tomatoes, puréed in a food processor
salt

Chop or slice the vegetables.

Heat the oil in a pan and sauté the onion until soft but not brown. Add the garlic and cook for a minute or two, taking care that it doesn't burn.

The next stage is very important. Add the spices, stirring and cooking them gently to 'mellow'. If the curry 'catches the throat' it's because the spices have not been mellowed to bring out their full flavour and to remove any harshness. Cook for approximately 3-4 minutes, taking care that they do not burn.

Add the vegetables and the canned tomatoes, including the tomato liquid. Season with salt. Cook over a medium heat until the vegetables are done.

Serves 8.

If you use a food processor, chopping the vegetables is easy. It's a good idea to make this dish in bulk and freeze.

Ghee is sometimes used instead of oil. Ghee is clarified butter which should be slowly cooked for about 45 minutes to impart a nutty flavour — but I can't see an Impatient Cook bothering!

Sambals for any curry dish

The good old favourite, finely chopped fresh tomato and onion.

Sliced banana sprinkled with lemon juice and then with chilli powder.

Finely chopped skinned cucumber in thick plain yoghurt.

Chutneys

Atchars

Coconut

Sultanas

Chopped pineapple and mango

Waldorf Salad

6 red-skinned eating apples
90 ml fresh lemon juice
5 stalks of table celery
60 g walnuts
1 lettuce
250 g cooked, diced chicken
mayonnaise or French dressing

Core and dice the apples. Sprinkle with lemon juice to prevent discoloration. Slice the celery coarsely and chop the walnuts. Wash the lettuce leaves and break into bite-sized pieces.

Line the serving bowl with the lettuce leaves. Mix the drained apple slices, celery, walnuts and chicken together in the mayonnaise or French dressing. Pile into the salad bowl on top of the lettuce leaves.

Yorkshire Pudding

Most newcomers to South Africa, and particularly to Johannesburg, battle with Yorkshire Pud. Instead of the pudding rising beautifully and getting stuck in the grill element of the oven, it ends up as a rather flat biscuit. Do not fear. There is a solution. Just double up on the egg content of your favourite recipe. And if you haven't got a favourite recipe, try mine.

125 g sifted cake flour
pinch of salt
2 jumbo eggs
250 ml very cold milk
50 ml ice-cold water

Place the flour and salt in a food processor or liquidiser/ blender. Turn on. Add the eggs and milk through the chute, blending until a smooth bubbly mixture is achieved. Let it stand for 1 hour. Place the bowl back on the machine and blend again, adding 50 ml ice-cold water.

Immediately pour into smoking hot individual Yorkshire pudding tins or into a smoking hot shallow oven dish. Either way, the containers should contain a little, very hot, oil or fat. Place at the top of a preheated oven at 220°C for 30-40 minutes (for the larger pud) or 25 minutes (for individual puds). Scale down the time if you are using very small tins.

Yorkshire Pudding should be well risen and crunchy golden on the outside and soft but cooked in the middle. As all ovens have their own difficult little ways, keep an eye on them the first time and, if necessary, turn the oven down to 200°C.

Makes 6-8 individual Yorkshire Puddings, depending on the size of the tins.

Just in case you are wondering about your meat, it needs to rest, covered with a tea-towel, in a warm place for 30 minutes before carving. It makes the carving process much easier and, of course, allows you to make delicious gravy from the juices.

Youngberry Mousse

*300 g youngberries**
200 ml sugar (as the fruit is often tart — but taste the fruit before adding the sugar)
20 ml gelatine
45 ml lemon juice
2 jumbo egg yolks
250 ml thick cream

*If you use canned youngberries you may find that they are extra sweet. If so, reduce or omit the sugar and sparkle up the fruit by adding 50 ml lemon juice.

Gently poach the washed youngberries with the sugar until cooked. There should be enough water adhering to the surface of the fruit to make the juice. Drain the fruit, reserving 150 ml of the juice. Heat the juice to boiling point.

Meanwhile, shake the measured gelatine on to the lemon juice in a small ramekin. Continue shaking the ramekin until the gelatine has been absorbed into the liquid. Leave for 1 minute to 'cake'. Microwave for approximately 30 seconds until translucent.

Place the fruit in a food processor and liquidise. Add the egg yolks. Continue blending, adding the boiling youngberry juice through the chute. Add the gelatine mixture. Blend for 1 minute. Add the cream with the machine blending continuously.

Pour into individual ramekins, cover with cling wrap and chill. Garnish with a rosette of cream and an uncooked youngberry.

Serves 8.

Iced Zabaglione

Worth the effort. The microwave makes it so quick.

6 jumbo egg yolks
180 g sugar
275 ml Marsala

Beat the egg yolks with the sugar until thick and light. Slowly mix in the Marsala.

Place the mixture in a microwave bowl and microwave on full power for 1 minute. Beat well. Microwave again on full power for 1 minute. Beat like mad. Continue giving 30-second blasts with mad whisks in between until the mixture has thickened.

Stand the bowl on the counter, and give the mixture a whisk every time you pass until it has cooled. Pour into ramekins. Cover and freeze.

Do not be tempted to leave the microwave during the whisking period as the mixture could curdle.

You can also make this dish in a bowl over a pan of boiling water, whisking the mixture continuously until it thickens. Have patience — it will take at least 20 minutes.

Serves 8.

FIBRE FAVOURITES

As is fairly obvious, The *Impatient Gourmet* is not a health book.

However, I do feel that fibre is often overlooked by the health-conscious cook. We watch our fat and sugar consumption and then forget that fibre can be another casualty of modern-day eating. The experts tell us that 30 g of fibre per day could be a healthy contribution in the prevention of many modern-day diseases.

The obvious way to eat sufficient fibre is with your breakfast cereal but do you always eat breakfast? Adding All-Bran Flakes* or Hi-Fibre Bran* to a delicious recipe makes certain of sufficient roughage to help protect your health — and give pleasure to your taste buds.

Either way, you can't lose!

By the way, if you have skipped that valuable breakfast, you can adapt many recipes in this book by adding between 20-50 g All-Bran Flakes*.

Contents

Apple and Lemony Pear Salad 82
Apricot Glazed Chicken 82

Baked Bran Bananas 82
Beef Pepperpot Soup 83
Bran Fruit Loaf 83
Bran Pita Bread 83

Cheesy Meatballs with Tomato and Herby Sauce 84
Chicken and Vegetable Crêpes 85
Chunky Courgette and Bean Soup 85
Citrus Impossible Pie 86
Crispy Bran Bars 86
Cucumber Boats with Chicken and Ham 86
Curried Bacon Flan 87

Fish Croquettes with Dill and Mustard Sauce 87

Lamb Julienne with Crispy Dumplings 88
Leek and Macaroni Cheese 88

Orange Delight 89
Orange-Marmalade Cake 89
Oriental Fried Fish 89

Smoked Angel-Fish Pâté 90
Smoked Haddock and Egg Flan 90
Spicy Apple Roll 94
Spicy Yoghurt Chicken Salad 94
Sunflower Tomatoes Stuffed with Tuna Salad 94

Yorkshire Lamb Chops 95

* All-Bran Flakes and Hi-Fibre Bran are registered trademarks of the Kellogg Company of South Africa

Apple and Lemony Pear Salad

125 ml thick natural yoghurt
5 ml lemon juice
15 ml parsley, chopped
2,5 ml salt
5 canned pear halves, drained well and sliced
2 red apples, cored and sliced (leave the skin on)
2 sticks celery, sliced
125 ml All-Bran Flakes, crushed*
red leaf lettuce
50 g pecans, chopped

Mix the yoghurt, lemon juice, parsley and salt. Stir in the pears and apples, coating well to prevent the apple discolouring. Cover with clingwrap and chill until ready to serve.

Just before serving, sprinkle with the All-Bran Flakes*.

Serve on red leaf lettuce, decorated with pecan nuts.

Serves 4

Apricot Glazed Chicken

The unusual balance of flavours with this dish is surprisingly delicious. The success of the dish lies in finding a good quality, chunky apricot jam.

150 g-200 g apricot jam — if you can't find chunky, use smooth mixed with chopped dried apricots that have been soaked for an hour or so.
60 ml mayonnaise
30 ml tomato sauce
5 ml grainy French mustard
8 boned, skinned breasts of chicken
30 ml butter
1 medium onion, chopped
1 stick celery, chopped
125 ml chicken stock
375 ml All-Bran Flakes
125 ml almonds, roughly chopped
salt and freshly ground black pepper
sprinkling of dried sage

Mix the jam, mayonnaise, tomato sauce and mustard. Leave to stand.

Meanwhile, place the chicken breast, cut side downwards, between either layers of waxed paper or plastic bags. Pound with a mallet, a rolling pin or a milk bottle to make the breasts thinner. Take care not to break the chicken flesh. Spread with jam mixture.

Melt the butter in a pan and sauté the onion until soft but not brown. Add the celery, cooking for a minute or two.

Mix the chicken stock and All-Bran Flakes* and allow to stand for a minute or two for the cereal to absorb the stock. Add the vegetables and the almonds, seasoning well. Add the sage. Stir well.

Roll up each breast and secure with cocktail sticks or poultry pins. The cocktail sticks or poultry pins are a bit messy to take out at the end but they do stop the filling coming out of the chicken breasts.

Place the breasts, seam side downwards, in a shallow baking dish and coat with the sauce.

Bake, covered with foil, at 180°C for about 30-40 minutes until the chicken is tender, removing the foil for the last 15 minutes.

Remember to remove the cocktail sticks or poultry pins.

Serves 4-8 depending on whether you want to serve 1 or 2 breasts per head — and on the size of the breasts.

Delicious with a mixture of wild and white rice and served with a salad.

Poultry pins are available at all good kitchen shops and last forever.

Baked Bran Bananas

4 bananas
200 ml strong coffee
125 ml dark rum
75 ml dark brown sugar
50 g All-Bran Flakes

Peel bananas and slice lengthways.

Place in shallow oven dish that just fits the length of the bananas.

Mix the coffee and dark rum together and pour over the bananas.

Mix the brown sugar and All-Bran Flakes* together and sprinkle over the top of the bananas.

Bake in a preheated oven at 180°C for about 20 minutes.

Serve with vanilla ice cream.

Serves 4

Beef Pepperpot Soup

This soup does take about 1 1/2 hours to cook (it depends on the cut of meat you use) but requires very little attention and makes a main meal.

300 g stewing beef, cut into cubes (I prefer boneless shin — it almost melts in the mouth when cooked sufficiently)
60 ml Worcestershire sauce
3 onions, sliced
6 carrots, sliced
2 sticks celery, sliced
20 ml tomato paste
sprinkling of sugar
10 ml smooth apricot jam
1/2 green pepper, seeded and diced
salt and freshly ground black pepper
Tabasco to taste
boiling water
*75 g All-Bran Flakes**
45 ml fresh parsley, chopped
125 ml pasta shapes
30 ml softened butter
30 ml flour

Put the cubes of beef in a plastic bag with the Worcestershire sauce, shaking well. Place in the fridge for half an hour or so turning occasionally.

Put the meat in a pan together with the Worcestershire Sauce, onions, carrots, celery, tomato paste, sugar, apricot jam, green pepper, seasoning and Tabasco to taste. Cover with boiling water. Stir well. Simmer, tightly covered, for 1 1/4-1 1/2 hours (depending on the cut of beef used) until the meat is tender.

Add the All-Bran Flakes*, parsley and pasta shapes. Cook for a further 10 minutes or until pasta is just cooked.

Mix the softened butter with the flour on a plate with a fork. Depending on how much you want to thicken the soup, take a little of the mixture and add it to the pan, spreading it on the side of the pan and then whisking it briskly into the hot mixture. This avoids lumps. The butter and flour mixture (beurre manie) must be 'cooked in' for a minute or so to mellow the taste of the flour and to thicken the soup. Add a little more if required.

Check the seasoning. If you like it a little hotter, add some more Tabasco and black pepper but remember, Tabasco adds fire and black pepper adds flavour!

Serves 4

Bran Fruit Loaf

*100 g All-Bran Flakes**
150 g sugar
275 g mixed dried fruit (but go heavy on the raisins and sultanas and light on the currants)
300 ml milk
100 g self-raising flour
pinch of salt

This is so easy that *anyone* can make it!

Mix the All-Bran Flakes*, sugar and dried fruit together. Mix well. Stir in milk and leave to stand for 30 minutes. Sieve the flour with the salt and stir into the mixture, stirring well.

Pour mixture into a well-greased loaf pan.

Bake in a preheated oven at 180°C for about an hour.

Turn out of tin immediately and cool on a rack.

Slice and spread with butter.

BE WARNED: When it comes out of the oven, it looks very, very moist and almost uncooked but dries out as it cools.

A great tea-time treat.

Bran Pita Bread

For Saturday lunch or Sunday supper, try taking left-over lean lamb, lettuce, tomato, chopped cucumber and thick natural yoghurt popped into a split pita bread pocket — with plenty of ground black pepper. It is delicious.

1 packet of active dried yeast (do check the expiry date before buying)
about 315 ml warm water (not hot)
*100 g All-Bran Flakes**, crushed*
380 ml bread flour
2,5 ml salt
65 ml oil
1 cup wholewheat flour

Dissolve the yeast in the warm water in the bowl of your electric mixer — remember, if the water is too hot, it could kill the yeast.

Add the All-Bran Flakes* and mix well.

On a low speed, add 1 cup of the bread flour, sifted with the salt, and the oil, mixing on high speed taking care to scrape down the sides of the bowl. Mix for 3 minutes.

The next stage can be done with a dough hook for your electric mixer but, if you don't have one, you can do it by hand.

Stir in the wholewheat flour and knead on low speed for 5 minutes or by hand, until the dough is smooth and elastic.

Only add the remaining bread flour if needed to make a smooth, manageable dough.

Divide the dough into 12 pieces and roll each piece in floured hands until it is a smooth ball. Cover with clingwrap for about 10 minutes.

On a well-floured board or counter, very lightly roll the ball, turning just once. You want to end up with a 15 cm round without creases or holes — and don't stretch the dough. It should go into a 15 cm round without any excessive pressure. Remember, you are not to thump with the rolling pin — very gently, please!

Place 3 pita breads on an ungreased baking sheet, taking care to keep them covered until ready for baking.

Bake in a preheated oven at 220°C. If you have any doubts about your oven's temperature, invest in an oven thermometer to hang on the oven shelf. You can adjust each recipe up or down if your oven isn't accurate.

Bake for about 4 minutes until the pita is puffed and slightly firm. Turn over and bake for a further 2 minutes until lightly brown. Cool on rack.

If you have a thermofan oven you can bake 2 or 3 trays at once. Should make 12 pita breads.

Pita Toast:

As a scrumptious alternative to hot toast or toast melba, split the pita bread horizontally. Place the pita bread, cut side upwards, on a baking tray. Spread with softened butter. Sprinkle with either sesame or poppy seeds. Bake in the oven at 140°C until golden brown. Store in a sealed container when cool. Delicious with pâté.

Cheesy Meatballs with Tomato and Herby Sauce

This dish can also be made with minced beef.

150 g minced pork
150 g minced veal
*100 g All-Bran Flakes**, crushed*
100 g mature Cheddar cheese, grated
2 eggs, lightly beaten
freshly ground black pepper

Mix all the ingredients together until just mixed.

Divide mixture into approx. 30 small balls. Roll each portion in lightly floured hands.

Place on baking sheet and bake in preheated oven at 200°C for about 15 minutes or until browned.

Meanwhile make:

Tomato and Herby Sauce:
350 g fresh tomatoes, seeded and chopped
1 onion, chopped
1/2 green pepper, seeded and chopped
1 stick celery, chopped
45 ml fresh orange juice
20 ml tomato paste
sprinkling of sugar
1 large, juicy clove of garlic, crushed
30 ml fresh coriander, chopped
30 ml fresh parsley, chopped
30 ml garlic chives, chopped
salt and freshly ground black pepper
generous pinch of sugar

Place fresh tomatoes, onion, green pepper, celery, orange juice, tomato paste, sugar and garlic in a small pan. Over a medium heat, cook until vegetables are just beginning to soften. Don't over-cook them as they will turn soggy. You need a little crispness in the final sauce. Take care to stir occasionally so that the mixture doesn't burn. Add the herbs. Season to taste. Add a pinch of sugar to counterbalance the acidity of the tomatoes. Cook for an additional couple of minutes, stirring well. If the mixture appears to be getting too dry, add a little more orange juice. If you are using a sweetened orange juice, omit the pinch of sugar.

When the cheesy meat balls come out of the oven, loosen them from the baking sheet with a palette knife.

Serve with the tomato and herby sauce and a tossed salad.

Serves 4

Chicken and Vegetable Crêpes

12 Crêpes:

See recipe on page 24 but reduce the flour to 100 g and add 25 g finely crushed All-Bran Flakes*.

250 ml broccoli, trimmed and cut into small florets
150 ml mushrooms, sliced
75 ml carrots, thinly sliced
The above amounts don't have to be that accurate
1/2 carton thick natural yoghurt
1/2 carton smooth cream cheese
60 ml fresh parsley, chopped
60 ml spring onions, chopped
375 ml cooked chicken, cut into slivers with the grain
*25 g Hi-Fibre Bran**
2,5 ml zest (rind) of lemon
salt and freshly ground black pepper
20 ml lemon juice
50 ml melted butter

Either cook the broccoli, mushrooms and carrots by your favourite method or steam them for about 8-10 minutes. They can also be microwaved but, whichever method you use, don't over-cook them and turn them soggy.

Take 1/2 carton yoghurt, the smooth cream cheese, 45 ml of the parsley, onions, garlic chives (if used), chicken, Hi-Fibre Bran*, lemon zest and seasoning and mix well. Gently mix in the vegetables.

Spoon the mixture onto each crêpe and roll up.

Take a large well-greased shallow baking dish and place the filled crêpes in it, seam side downwards (so they won't unroll in the oven).

Bake in a preheated oven at 180°C for about 12 minutes or until thoroughly heated.

Remove from the oven and pour over lemon juice mixed with melted butter.

Serves 4-6

Chunky Courgette and Bean Soup

30 ml oil
50 g butter
125 g streaky bacon, cut into slivers
325 g potatoes, peeled and diced
325 g courgettes, thickly sliced
325 g leeks, chopped
1 can kidney beans
1 clove garlic, crushed
1 litre chicken stock (instant is fine but go easy on the salt)
freshly ground black pepper
2,5 ml dried basil
*50 g Hi-Fibre Bran**
45 ml fresh parsley, chopped
Cheddar cheese and fresh parsley for garnish

Heat the oil and butter and fry the bacon until crisp. Remove with slotted spoon and drain on paper towel.

Sauté the potatoes, courgettes and leeks for 4-5 minutes.

Remove with slotted spoon and place in a pan together with the bacon.

Add the kidney beans, complete with liquid from the can together with garlic, chicken stock, pepper, basil, Hi-Fibre Bran* and parsley.

Bring to the boil and simmer until the vegetables are just cooked.

Check the seasoning. It is unlikely to need additional salt but it might need some additional pepper.

Serve sprinkled with grated Cheddar cheese and a little additional chopped parsley.

Serves 4-6

Citrus Impossible Pie

This recipe seems too simple to be true — but it WORKS!

4 jumbo eggs
250 ml sugar
125 ml butter, melted
100 g slivered almonds
250 ml desiccated coconut
*250 ml All-Bran Flakes**
grated zest (rind) 2 oranges and approx. 125 ml juice
grated zest (rind) 2 lemons and approx. 125 ml juice
250 ml milk
125 ml cake flour, sifted

Just place all the ingredients in a food processor and blend for 1 minute. Take care not to overblend. Yes, truly — that's all you have to do.

Pour the mixture into a well-greased 28 cm pie dish and bake in a preheated oven at 180°C. Bake for about an hour or until golden brown on top.

Remove from the oven. Serve warm.

Sprinkle with castor sugar and a little additional coconut.

The left-over pie takes reheating — in fact, on one occasion I was a trifle forgetful and the pie got a trifle dark but everyone loved the crunchy topping!

If you want to be wicked, serve it with thick, thick cream and some additional orange segments.

Crispy Bran Bars

Everyone feels like indulging in a sweet treat at some time or other.

Get some of your valuable bran intake at the same time.

150 g butter
150 g marshmallows
150 g caramel toffee, broken into pieces
*150 g All-Bran Flakes**

Melt the butter, marshmallows and caramel toffee together in a pan and boil for 1-2 minutes.

Remove from the heat.

Stir in the All-Bran Flakes*.

Spread into a buttered Swiss roll tin and leave to set.

Cut into 12 squares and then eat!

Unfortunately, it won't last long!

Cucumber Boats With Chicken and Ham

A great pre-dinner snack which is different.

4-5 small cucumbers
60 g cooked chicken
60 g ham
1 anchovy fillet
mayonnaise (preferably my recipe on page 42)
*50 g All-Bran Flakes**
watercress for garnish

Take a fork and score down the outside skins of the cucumbers.

Cut slices about 2½-3 cm thick. Cut the slices in half.

Scoop out the middle so you are left with open-ended boats.

If the cucumber is a bit coarse, plunge into boiling salted water for a few minutes. Drain and refresh under cold water.

Coarsely chop the chicken, ham and anchovy.

Place in a food processor together with sufficient mayonnaise to make a smooth mixture.

Add the All-Bran Flakes* and blend for a few seconds to mix but take care not to overblend as the flakes will add a texture to the mixture.

If using shop-bought mayonnaise, additional pepper will be needed but probably not salt due to the anchovy fillet.

Spoon into the cucumber boats.

Garnish with sprigs of watercress.

Curried Bacon Flan

Pastry:
150 g cake flour
pinch of salt
*25 g All-Bran Flakes**
80 g butter
iced water

Filling:
30 g butter
125 g celery, sliced thinly
125 g streaky bacon, diced
5 ml curry powder
3 eggs, beaten
175 ml thick natural yoghurt
salt and freshly ground black pepper
2 medium tomatoes, thinly sliced

Place the cake flour, salt and All-Bran Flakes* in the processor with the metal blade and turn on. Add the cold butter, cut into pieces, through the chute. Blend until breadcrumb stage. Add just sufficient water to make a firm dough. Chill for 30 minutes and then roll out to line a 20 cm flan dish.

Prick the bottom of the flan and bake 'blind' in a preheated oven at 200°C for approx. 15 minutes.

Melt the butter in a small frying pan and sauté the celery and bacon until golden brown.

Stir in the curry powder and cook for 2 minutes to 'mellow'. Mix the eggs with the yoghurt. Add the pan ingredients and season to taste. Turn into the flan case.

Top with tomato slices.

Bake in a preheated oven at 190°C for about 25 minutes until golden brown and set.

Serves 4

Fish Croquettes with Dill and Mustard Sauce

With this recipe, you can use canned tuna or salmon.

Croquettes:
*175 ml All-Bran Flakes**
5 ml oil
1 can tuna or salmon (approx. 185 g size), drained and flaked
30 ml onion, chopped finely
1 small stick celery, chopped finely
60 ml parsley, chopped
2 eggs, lightly beaten
10 ml lemon juice
freshly ground black pepper

Dill and mustard sauce:
30 ml flour
salt
5 ml fresh dill, chopped
or 2.5 ml dried dill
250 ml milk
10 ml grainy French mustard
15 ml lemon juice

Crush half the All-Bran Flakes* by either placing in a plastic bag and rolling with rolling pin or in a food processor. Mix half the All-Bran crumbs with oil and reserve.

Mix the remaining cereal with the fish, onion, celery, parsley, eggs and lemon juice until thoroughly mixed, seasoning well with the black pepper.

Shape into 4 croquettes and roll in the All-Bran crumbs and oil mixture until coated.

Place on a baking sheet and bake in a preheated oven at 180°C for about 25 minutes.

Make the sauce by mixing the flour, salt, dill, milk and mustard in a pan, beating until smooth. Cook over a medium heat until bubbly and thickening, stirring constantly.

Stir in the lemon juice.

Serve over the hot fish croquettes.

Serves 2-4

Lamb Julienne with Crispy Dumplings

Although this dish takes 2 hours or so to cook, the actual preparation time is quite short especially if you get the butcher to cut up the meat! A really great winter dish.

about 75 ml flour
5-10 ml curry powder (according to taste)
10 ml salt
freshly ground black pepper
750 g stewing lamb, off the bone and cut into cubes
oil
750 ml chicken stock
12 pickling onions, skinned
8 carrots, sliced

Mix the flour, curry powder, salt and freshly ground black pepper together. Place in a plastic bag together with the meat cubes and shake around to coat the meat evenly.

Fry the meat in hot oil until browned.

If there is any excess flour left over, stir in a little.

You shouldn't have surplus oil left in the pan.

Gradually add the hot stock, stirring well. Transfer to a large casserole, adding the onions and carrots. Cover. Cook in a preheated oven at 180°C for about an hour. Adjust the seasoning.

Crispy Dumplings:
40 g butter
125 ml fresh white breadcrumbs
50 ml All-Bran Flakes, lightly crushed*
150 g self-raising flour
sprinkling salt
2,5 ml dehydrated onions
30 ml oil
milk

Melt the butter in a pan and stir in the crumbs and All-Bran Flakes*, stirring frequently until crumbs are golden.

Sift the flour and salt together and then add the dehydrated onion. Stir in the oil and enough milk to give a soft but manageable dough. Shape into balls and arrange in the lamb casserole. Replace lid and cook for a further hour but don't take off the lid during this time.

The cooking time will be determined by the cut of lamb you use.

Serves 6

Leek and Macaroni Cheese

125 g macaroni
60 g butter
250 g leeks, roughly chopped
30 g flour
400 ml milk
150 ml cream
175 g Cheddar cheese, grated
salt and freshly ground black pepper
sprinkling of cayenne pepper
25 g All-Bran Flakes, coarsely crushed*
30 ml chives or garlic chives, chopped
2,5 ml paprika

Cook the macaroni in a pan of fast boiling salted water until tender but not soft. Drain well.

Melt the butter in a pan and sauté the leeks for a couple of minutes. Stir in the flour and 'mellow' for a minute or two, stirring constantly. Add the milk, a little at a time, stirring well to avoid lumps. Bring to the boil and simmer for 2-3 minutes, stirring constantly. Add the cream. Stir.

Remove from the heat and stir in the macaroni and most of the cheese (saving about 30 ml). Season to taste, adding a sprinkling of cayenne.

Spoon the mixture into a buttered 1 litre shallow ovenproof dish.

Mix the All-Bran Flakes* and rest of cheese together.

Sprinkle in lines across the dish. Add a little paprika for colour.

Bake in a preheated oven at 190°C for 30-35 minutes, until golden.

Sprinkle with chopped chives or garlic chives as garnish.

Serves 4

Orange Delight

300 ml milk
1 orange
knob of butter (about 15 g)
30 g sugar
*50 g All-Bran Flakes**, crushed*
2 jumbo eggs
100 g icing sugar
mint leaves to decorate

Heat the milk, grated zest (rind) of the orange and knob of butter together in a pan. Add the 30 g sugar and All-Bran Flakes*.

Separate the eggs and add the yolks to the mixture, mixing well. Pour into a buttered ovenproof dish (approx. 750 ml capacity). Bake in a preheated oven at 170°C for approximately 20 minutes. Remove from the oven. Top with orange segments. Whisk the egg whites until stiff. Very gently fold in a couple of spoons of the icing sugar.

Then gently fold in the rest. Pile meringue over pudding.

Brown in a hot oven or under the grill.

Decorate with mint sprigs.

Serves 4

Orange-Marmalade Cake

Very much a 'winter warmer'. Serve warm as a dessert with ice-cream or as a teatime special with whipped cream.

150 ml marmalade
3-4 oranges, skinned and cut into segments
100 ml brown sugar
30 ml flour
125 ml cake flour
125 ml wholewheat flour
75 ml sugar
10 ml baking powder
2,5 ml salt
2,5 ml nutmeg
*250 ml All-Bran Flakes**
250 ml milk
1 egg, lightly beaten
65 ml butter, softened

Spread the marmalade over the bottom of a greased 20 cm round cake tin. Mix the orange segments, brown sugar and flour together. Arrange neatly over the marmalade.

Sift the cake flour, wholewheat flour, sugar, baking powder, salt and nutmeg. Then return the pieces left over from the wholewheat flour to the sifted mixture. The sieving of the flour really does make the cake lighter.

Put the All-Bran Flakes* and milk together in a jug. Mix well and leave to stand for 2-3 minutes so that the cereal can soften. Add the egg and butter, mixing well.

Add the flour mixture to the cereal mixture, taking care to stir it only sufficiently to mix the ingredients.

Spread over the oranges.

Bake in a preheated oven at 200°C for approx. 25 minutes or until the cake is golden brown and springy to the touch.

Remove from oven and serve.

Oriental Fried Fish

4 fillets of Cape Whiting (or any white firm fish)
thick, dark soy sauce — 5 ml per fillet
sprinkling of ground ginger
flour
salt and freshly ground black pepper
1 jumbo egg
150 ml desiccated coconut
100 ml white breadcrumbs
*50 ml All-Bran Flakes**, crushed*
oil
butter
litchis
2 bananas, sliced

Sprinkle the fish with soy sauce. Sprinkle with a little ginger. Leave for 15 minutes.

Season the flour with salt and freshly ground black pepper and roll the fillets in it.

Beat the egg and dip the fillets in it. Mix the coconut, breadcrumbs and All-Bran Flakes* together.

Roll the fillets in the mixture, pressing it carefully all over them.

Heat a few spoonfuls of oil in a pan and when it is hot, add a generous knob of butter. When it is melted, fry the fillets in it for approx. 4-5 minutes on each side over a moderate heat.

The actual time will depend on the thickness of the fillets.

Serve with litchis (canned are fine) and sliced bananas added to the pan for the last 5 minutes.

Serve with boiled baby potatoes tossed in parsley accompanied by the apple and lemony pear salad (see page 83).

Serves 2-4, depending on size of fillets.

Smoked Angel-Fish Pâté

Smoked mackerel can be substituted but good smoked angel-fish is fairly easily obtainable and has a superb flavour.

250 g smoked angel-fish
*25 g All-Bran Flakes**
30 ml milk
60 g butter, melted
30 ml lemon juice
5 ml grated lemon zest (rind)
150 ml thick natural yoghurt
60 ml smooth cottage cheese
15 ml cream of horseradish
black pepper to taste

Blend all the ingredients together in a food processor.

Place in a pâté dish and cover with clingwrap. Chill well.

Serve garnished with lemon slices and some fennel greenery.

Delicious with Pita toast (see page 85)

Smoked Haddock and Egg Flan

This recipe is only for the Impatient Gourmet if you have some leftover potatoes from Sunday lunch — or you could use the instant variety but jazz it up with some cream, pepper and a touch of nutmeg.

Impatient Gourmets make a number of pastry shells at one time — when they are in the mood — and freeze them uncooked (ready for quick action in the kitchen). I have also frozen leftover creamed potato successfully as well as little dishes of leftover white sauce. It makes life much easier if you don't have to start from scratch!

Do label properly though. Otherwise you will end up with mystery frozen offerings that you will never use — I speak from the heart as it has happened to me.

Pastry:
300 g cake flour
pinch of salt
*50 g All-Bran Flakes**
150 g butter
iced water

Filling:
450 g smoked haddock fillets, cooked and flaked
8 spring onions, chopped
2 hard boiled eggs, sliced
375 ml white sauce (see recipe on page 64)
450 g creamed potato
120 g grated Cheddar cheese
*50 g All-Bran Flakes**

Place the cake flour, salt and All-Bran Flakes* in a food processor using the metal blade. Turn on, adding pieces of cold butter through the chute. Blend until breadcrumb stage. Blend for a few seconds and add sufficient iced water to make firm dough. DON'T OVERMIX!

Roll out and line 2 x 20 cm flan dishes. Prick the bottoms of the flans. Chill.

Bake in preheated oven at 200°C for 20-25 minutes.

Place the flaked fish in the pastry cases and top with spring onions and sliced eggs.

Pour over the well-flavoured white sauce.

Top with creamed potatoes.

Sprinkle with cheese and All-Bran Flakes*.

Bake in preheated oven at 200°C for about 30 minutes until brown.

Opposite: Smoked Angel-Fish Pâté.
Overleaf: Apple and Lemony Pear Salad.

Spicy Apple Roll

Do make certain that the cinnamon and nutmeg are still full of flavour — check their fragrant smell. If it has gone, so has the flavour.

Pastry:
225 g cake flour
pinch of salt
125 g butter
1 egg
iced water

Filling:
450 g apples, peeled, cored and sliced (canned ones are fine)
*50 g All-Bran Flakes**
2,5 ml ground cinnamon
2,5 ml ground nutmeg
grated zest (rind) of 1 lemon
grated zest (rind) of 1 orange
50 g butter
75 g brown sugar
75 g sultanas

Make the pastry by rubbing the cold butter into the sieved flour and salt. Add the egg and small amount of iced water to make a smooth, firm dough. Chill for 30 minutes.

Roll out to a rectangle about 38 cm x 25 cm.

Place on baking sheet. Brush pastry with melted butter. Mix the remaining ingredients together and spoon over the pastry. Roll up like a Swiss roll.

Brush the top with the rest of the melted butter.

Bake in a preheated oven at 230° for 15 minutes and then reduce the heat to 190°C for a further 15-20 minutes.

It is delicious hot or cold but if you would like to gild the lily, add a few segments of orange to the apples.

Delicious with vanilla ice-cream.

Previous page: Bran Fruit Loaf

Spicy Yoghurt Chicken Salad

This salad makes a great Saturday luncheon dish served with hot French bread. It stretches the chicken too!

175 ml thick natural yoghurt
2.5 ml salt
freshly ground black pepper
2.5 ml-5 ml curry paste — to taste. (The strength of the curry paste will determine the amount used. Curry paste is better than curry powder in dishes that are not going to be cooked)
pinch ground ginger
1 bunch spring onions, chopped
30 ml garlic chives, chopped
1/2 green pepper, seeded and chopped
2 sticks celery, chopped
small bunch of black or green grapes, halved and seeded
3 cooked breasts of chicken, skinned and diced
*50 g All-Bran Flakes**
red leaf lettuce
watercress

Mix the yoghurt, salt, pepper, curry paste and ginger together. Gently mix the spring onions, garlic chives, green pepper, celery, most of the grapes, chicken and All-Bran Flakes* into the mixture. Cover and chill well.

Serve on lettuce leaves, garnished with grapes and watercress.

Serves 4

Sunflower Tomatoes Stuffed with Tuna Salad

60 ml Mayonnaise
60 ml thick natural yoghurt
generous pinch dried dill or finely chopped fresh dill
zest of 1 lemon (grated outer yellow skin)
100 g cucumber, chopped with its skin on
1/2 bunch radishes, sliced
1 bunch spring onions, chopped
30 ml parsley, chopped

salt and freshly ground black pepper
*50 g Hi-Fibre Bran**
300 g canned tuna, drained well and flaked
8 medium-sized tomatoes

Stir the mayonnaise, yoghurt, dill and lemon zest together. Add the cucumber, radishes, spring onions and parsley. Season to taste. Stir well.

Add the Hi-Fibre Bran and tuna, tossing gently to mix. Don't overmix and turn it into a sloshy mess!

With the stalk side of the tomatoes on the chopping board, slice the tomatoes downwards ALMOST, BUT NOT QUITE TO THE BOTTOM MAKING 6 SEGMENTS. Push the segments outwards so that the tomato opens up into a flower shape but is anchored at the bottom.

Place the mixture in the middle. Serve tomatoes on a bed of lettuce, decorated with additional slices of celery and lemon and topped with a sprig of dill.

Serves 8 as a starter or 4 as a lunch-time salad.

Yorkshire Lamb Chops

8 lamb chops
60 ml All-Bran Flakes, crushed*
salt and freshly ground black pepper
60 g Cheddar cheese, grated
60 g butter
2 onions, finely sliced
300 ml milk
30 g flour
30 ml cream

Grill the chops, under a hot grill, on one side only. Meanwhile, mix the All-Bran Flakes*, salt and freshly ground black pepper and cheese together.

Turn the chops over and top with the bran mixture, dotting with a little butter. Continue to grill until thoroughly cooked.

While the chops are grilling, boil the onions in the milk until softening.

Melt the remaining butter in a pan, stir in the flour and cook gently for a minute or two. Stir in the milk and onions, whisking well to avoid lumps. Bring back to the boil and continue to cook, stirring constantly, until the sauce slightly thickens. Stir in the cream and season well. Pour the sauce over the chops.

Be careful to avoid burning — the All-Bran Flakes* can 'catch' quickly.

Allowing 2 chops per person, serves 4

* All-Bran Flakes and Hi-Fibre Bran are registered trademarks of the Kellogg Company of South Africa

Index

Amaretto Cream with Plum Purée 1
Anchovy
Butter 65
Crescents 21
Apple
and Cointreau Pots 1
and Lemony Pear Salad 82
Roll, Spicy 94
Soup, Curried 69
Stuffed, Salad 1
Apricot Glazed Chicken 82
Artichokes and Mangetout with Blue Cheese Dressing 42
Asparagus
and Cheese Charlotte 2
with Yoghurt Dressing 2
Avocado
Baked 2
with Blue Cheese Dressing 3
Guacamole 3
Mousse 3

Bacon
and Cheese Potato Cakes 13
and Potato Omelette 52
and Prune Rolls 21
Baked Beans, Old-fashioned, with Ham Chunks 5
Baked Bran Bananas 82
Bananas, Brazilian 5
Barbequed Spare Ribs 71
Batters *see* Crispy Coatings
Beef
Boeuf Stroganoff 7
Corned, Hash 5
Fillet 6
Fillet, with Mustard Sauce 6
Pepperpot Soup 83
Roast, with Gravy 6
Blue Cheese Dressing, with Avocado 3
Bolognese Sauce 62
Bran
Bars, Crispy 86
Fruit Loaf 83
Pita Bread 83
Brandy
Butter 7
Truffles 7
Bread
Easy 8
Easy Yoghurt 8
Sauce 63
Spicy Marmalade 8
Breakfast Muffins 45
Brie, Fruit 35
Burgers Stroganoff 11
Butter
Brandy 7
Savoury, *see* Savoury Butters

Cabbage, Savoury 12
Camembert Ice-Cream 38
Casserole
Vegetable 77
Caviar Balls 21
Celery
and Apricot and Pecan Stuffing 76
and Mushrooms with Wild Rice 60
Snack 22
Champagne Sauce 63
Charlotte
Asparagus and Cheese 2
Katrine 12
Cheese
and Asparagus Charlotte 2
and Bacon Potato Cake 13
Omelette 52
Pastry 54
Cheesecake, Shirley's 13
Cheesy Meatballs with Tomato and Herby Sauce 84
Cherries Jubilee 13
Cherry Tomatoes, with Smoked Snoek Pâté 21
Chestnut Stuffing 76
Chicken
Hotpot 13
Moroccan 14
with Oranges 14
Patties, with Pineapple and Ham 37
and Potato Cakes 15
Salad 15
Tonnato 15
and Vegetable Crêpes 85
with Whisky Cream Sauce 16
Chicken Liver
Kebabs, Devilled 17
Omelette 52
Pâté 16
Sauté 16
Chilli con Carne 17
Chips, Golden Crunchy 56
Chocolate, melting 17
Cloud 18
Fridge Cake 18
Ganache Cream 19
Sauce 64

Christmas
Fritters 20
Pudding 19
Pudding, Fried with Preserved Figs 20
Chunky Courgette and Bean Soup 85
Citrus Impossible Pie 86
Cocktail Party Food 20
Coconut Crunchies 22
Coffee Meringue Gâteau 23
Corned Beef Hash 5
Courgettes, Instant 23
Couscous 23
Cranberry Orange Relish 64
Crème Brûlée, Easy 77
Crépes 24
Crépes Suzette 24
Crispy Bran Bars 86
Crispy Coatings 25
Croques Monsieur 25
Cucumber Boats with Chicken and Ham 86
Cumberland Sauce 64
Curried Apple Soup 69
Curried Bacon Flan 87
Curried Turkey Soup 69
Curry
Kingklip 40
Vegetable 77

Dessert, Delectable 26
Devilled Chicken Liver Kebabs 17
Devilled Kidneys 39
Devilled Pork 55
Devilled Prawns, with Egg Mousse 32
Dressings
Blue Cheese 3, 42
Parsley and Walnut 26
Salad 31
Sherry 31
Sweet Pepper 31
Tomato and Yoghurt 31
Yoghurt 2

Easy Bread 8
Easy Crême Brûlée 77
Easy Quiche 59
Easy Yoghurt Loaf 8
Egg Mousse with Devilled Prawns 32
Eggs
Framed 32
Poached 32
Scotch Surprise 33
Scrambled 33

Figs, Preserved, with Fried Christmas Pudding 20
Fillet of Beef 6
with Mustard Sauce 6
Fish
Croquettes with Dill and Mustard Sauce 87
Flaming 35
Oriental 34, 89
Parcels 34
Platter 34
Florentinas 35
French Onion Soup 70
Fridge Cake, Chocolate 18
Fritters, Christmas 20
Fruit Brie 35
Fruit Crumble 35
Fruit Salad
Special 36
Winter, with Cottage Cheese 36
Fudge Sundae, Hot 37

Garlic Butter 65
Gâteau, Coffee Meringue 23
Grapes, Stuffed 22
Grilled Lamb Cutlets, with Gooseberry and Apple Sauce 37

Haddock and Smoked Mussel Pâté 66
Ham and Pineapple Chicken Patties 37
Hash, Corned Beef 5
Hot Fudge Sundae 37

Ice-Cream
Ann's Easy 38
Camembert 38

Jacket Baked Onions 38

Kassler Chops, Quick Recipe 39
Kebabs, Devilled Chicken Liver 17
Kedgeree 39
Kidneys, Devilled 39
Kingklip Curry 40

Lamb Cutlets, with Gooseberry and Apple Sauce 37
Lamb Julienne with Crispy Dumplings 88
Leek and Macaroni Cheese 88
Lemon Meringue Pie 41
Lemon and Orange Water Ice 53
Liver and Onion Bake 41

Mangetout and Artichokes with Blue Cheese Dressing 42
Mangoes, Flaming 42
Marmalade Bread, Spicy 8
Mayonnaise 42

Melon, Spiced 43
Meringues, My Never-Fail 43
Minced Pies 44
Mousse
  Avocado 3
  Egg, with Devilled Prawns 32
  Smoked Salmon 69
  Youngberry 79
Muffins, Breakfast 45
Mushroom Omelette 52
Mushrooms
  à la Greque 45
  and Celery with Wild Rice 60
Mussels
  In Curry Cream Sauce 46
  Smoked, and Haddock Pâté 66
Mustard Sauce, with Fillet of Beef 6

Nectarine Dessert 51
Noodles, Nutty 51

Old-fashioned Baked Beans with Ham Chunks 5
Omelettes
  Bacon and Potato 52
  Cheese 52
  Chicken Liver 52
  Mushrooms 52
  Plain 52
  Tomato 53
Onion and Liver Bake 41
Onions, Jacket Baked 38
Orange and Lemon Water Ice 53
Orange Delight 89
Orange-Marmalade Cake 89
Oriental Fried Fish 89
Oxford Cream 53

Paella 54
Parsley Butter 66
Party Drinks 22
Pasta, Roquefort 61
Pastry
  Cheese 54
  Shortcrust 55
Pâté
  Chicken Liver 16
  Roquefort Cheese 60
  Smoked Angel-Fish 90
  Smoked Mussel and Haddock 66
Pineapple, Ham and Chicken Patties 37
Plum Purée, with Amaretto Cream 1
Poached Eggs 32
Pork
  Chops, Stuffed 56
  Devilled 55
  Fillet, Instant Dinner 56
Potato and Bacon Omelette 52
Potato Cakes
  with Bacon and Cheese 13
  with Chicken 15
Potatoes
  Château 56
  Delicious Roasties 57
  Golden Crunchy Chips 56
  Mish-Mash 57
  Spicy Fries 58
  Tuna-stuffed 57
Prawn Salpicon 58
Prawns
  Devilled, with Egg Mousse 32
  Peri-Peri 58
Prune and Bacon Rolls 21
Pudding
  Christmas 19
  Yorkshire 79
Pumpkin and Tomato Soup 70

Quiche, Easy 59
Quickie Kassler Chops 39

Ratatouille 59
Relish, Cranberry Orange 64
Rice
  Dirty 59
  Nutty Cheesy 60
  Wild, with Mushrooms and Celery 60
Roast Beef and Delicious Gravy 6
Roasting the Christmas Turkey 75
Roquefort Cheese Pâté 60
Roquefort Pasta 61

Salads
  Chicken 15
  Stuffed Apple 1
  Waldorf 78
Salami Cornets 22
Salmon Soup 70
Salmon, Smoked
  Canapés 21
  Mousse 69
Salpicon, Prawn 58
Sambals 78
Sardine Oblongs 22
Sauces
  Béarnaise 62

Béchamel *see* Sauces, White
Bologneses 62
Bread 63
Champagne 63
Chocolate 64
Cumberland 64
Curry Cream 46
Gooseberry and Apple 37
Mustard 6
Whisky Cream 16
White 64
Savoury Butters
Anchovy 65
Garlic 65
Parsley 66
Topping for Grilled Steak 65
Savoury Cabbage 12
Scrambled Eggs 33
Shortcrust Pastry 55
Smoke Cookery 66
Smoked Angel-Fish Pâté 90
Smoked Haddock and Egg Flan 90
Smoked Mussel and Haddock Pâté 66
Smoked Salmon Mousse 69
Soups
Curried Apple 69
Curried Turkey 69
French Onion 70
Pumpkin and Tomato 70
Salmon 70
Spare Ribs, Barbequed 71
Spiced Melon 43
Spicy Apple Roll 94
Spicy Fries 58
Spicy Marmalade Bread 8
Spicy Yoghurt Chicken Salad 94
Steak Tartare 21
Strawberry Phyllo Surprise 71
Stuffed Apple Salad 1
Stuffed Grapes 22
Stuffed Pork Chops 56
Stuffed Tomatoes 74
Stuffings
Couscous 23
see also Turkey Stuffings

Sunflower Tomatoes 74
Sunflower Tomatoes Stuffed with Tuna Salad 94
Syllabub 71

Taramasalata 73
Toad-in-the-hole 73
Toast Melba 73
Tomato
Braai Special 74
Omelette 53
and Pumpkin Soup 70
Tomatoes
Stuffed 74
Sunflower 74
Torrijas 74
Trifle 75
Trout Père Louis 75
Truffles, Brandy 7
Tuna-stuffed Potatoes 57
Turkey
Christmas, Roasting of 75
Curried, Soup 69
Turkey Stuffings
Celery, Apricot and Pecan 76
Chestnut 76

Unbelievably Easy Crème Brûlée 77

Vegetable
Casserole 77
Curry 77

Waldorf Salad 78
Water Ice, Orange and Lemon 53
White Sauce 64

Yoghurt
Chicken Salad 94
Dressing, with Asparagus 2
Loaf, Easy 8
Yorkshire Lamb Chops 95
Yorkshire Pudding 79
Youngberry Mousse 79

Zabaglione, Iced 79